Mob

MOBILIZE!

DANCING IN THE WORLD

CHAUNCEY BELL

Published by Harvester Press

ISBN 979-8-6900-7279-7

Foreword

Chauncey Bell has been one of my closest and most cherished collaborators for 40 years. Soon after my arrival in the U.S., Chauncey became one of my first students and then became an indispensable collaborator in the design, invention, and delivery of the work I was doing with corporations.* The drift of my own life and career have been deeply touched by his care and involvement.

Chauncey's talent for design and generosity of spirit cannot be separated from his sensibility for what it means to be human: in conversation, in conflict, in love, in service, in dreaming the future, in the inheritance of past traditions, and in the celebration of co-creation. Sometimes, I detect all of this in Chauncey's spontaneous, magnanimous laughter. I detect this too in his capacity to locate and design ways out of what he calls the messes that organizations get themselves into.

The collection of texts Chauncey has put together here are a gift to future generations of designers, coaches, consultants, thinkers, seekers, and wanderers. Anyone involved in bringing forth important projects and enterprises would be wise to call on Chauncey and to draw from what he has provided in the texts that follow. His singular voice will continue to be a source of possibilities for others navigating an indefinite horizon.

Fernando L. Flores
Founder of Pluralistic Networks
Co-Author of Understanding Computers and Cognition: A New Foundation for Design

*CEMEX, IBM, Citibank, AT&T, ABB, CVS, Trans-Alta Utilities, TELMEX, Codelco, and others.

Preface

I wrote the essays in this and the volumes that follow with colleagues in the midst of work with clients and friends over a period of a half a century. Life has taken me deeply into developing new ways of working in many worlds, including:

- The governance of major corporations

- The functioning of networked technology

- The manufacture of semiconductors and biotechnological sub-stances

- Management of Western city, state, and national governments, in-cluding criminal justice systems

- The work of public and private institutions involved with the care of our bodies.

It has been a privilege to witness the way that people in these very different worlds confront and struggle with historical messes every day. I have asked myself why I have been invited into these worlds. In part I guess it is because people have glimpsed that I have been working with powerful questions and with a dogged commitment to dig into terrain that we human beings think we understand well but actually do not.

Life is full of mysteries. Over the years, fabulous mentors, teachers, colleagues, friends, wives and children have been constant sources of inspiration. The moments of inspiration have not always been lovely. Many times insights, possibilities, and opportunities have emerged from situations that were initially unpleasant. I would find myself unsettled, uncomfortable, irritated, or downright angry and then would recognize that yet another interruption might be opening a new opportunity. We begin to learn to ride a bicycle by falling off it and getting back on over and over.

Recently the human beings on this planet entered a new era shaped in important ways by the COVID-19 pandemic, a humbling disruption from which we are forced to learn.

"Epidemics are a category of disease that seem to hold up the mirror to human beings as to who we really are. ... epidemics have shaped history in part because they've led human beings inevitably to think about philosophical, religious, and moral issues."

–Isaac Chotiner, in the New Yorker, March 3, 2020

Day by day, we get new evidence of the shallowness of our thinking as human beings. We think we can predict the future in a changing world. We are addicted to assigning causes and effects in our worlds. And we are incompetent at the job of moving from our current world to a new world of our own design. These should be wake-up calls. My wife, Shirah, is fond of Andre Gide's expression: "In order to discover new lands, one must be willing to lose sight of the shore for a very long time." COVID-19 has taken us out of sight of the shore, opened our eyes to many features of our old worlds that are deficient or damaged, and invited us to explore the possibility of building bridges to new worlds.

Later in these essays I will speculate that the capacity to bring new practices may well be the most important competence we have to develop in the era in which we find ourselves. The path from our current world to a new one will not be reliably found through management, nor innovation, nor leadership. Nor will a reliable path be found in technology, academia, politics, religion, or spiritual studies. While all of these are important for making needed transitions, none reliably open spaces in which we will find ourselves in a new world.

The quality of my life has had a great deal to do with the many gifts I have received. I talk about those gifts in various ways in my essays. This first volume is devoted to introducing my work and career, myself as an observer, and the foundations on which I stand. Subsequent volumes will include essays centered on topics including:

- Designing Enterprises

- Mapping and Orchestrating Coordination

- Human Dark Matter: Identifying Coordination Waste

- The Practice of Bringing New Practices

- Care of our Bodies in this 'Modern' World

- Reflections of this God-Fearing Atheist

- Moving beyond the Financialization of Everything

My life has been filled with wonderful human beings, many gifts, opportunities, challenges, joy, wonder and awe. I have married lovely, proud, estimable women who have been kind to me. I have been alive for 76 years. Early in 2019 I had an ischemic stroke in the left parietal region of the brain. After that, as I moved to redesign how I would manage my calendar, scheduling, and the other pieces of my work, Laurie Dent, my assistant and friend for many years, fed me my own medicine: "Don't be silly," she said, "everything you do emerges from your relationships with other human beings. Handle that and the rest will take care of itself." In May of this year I became bionic when my doctors replaced my left hip with titanium, glass, and polyurethane. I have chosen to understand these events as opportunities to rethink how I invest myself in what I care about.

What I say in the following is emphatically subjective. Those of us on the planet are currently finishing our dwelling in an era in which 'objective' truths, laws, and evidence ruled the day. In this era, science (for many people) has grown to the proportions of a new religion, often replacing the thousands of years-old traditions in which we looked to the heavens for guidance about how to live with each other. We have arrived in an era in which our capacity to think beyond what we can see and what we just heard someone say is drastically limited.

If, for example, we are concerned with inequalities in our social spaces, our traditions teach us to focus on indicators – 'evidence' – to suggest which side of an argument we should attend to. The argumentative style we have come to accept as an appropriate way of encountering each other rarely triggers new questions about what we are doing. Inequality? The vast inequalities confronting our societies mean that we are living in the midst of serious dangers not revealed by 'objective' indicators. What kind of education are we providing the next generations to support them in sustaining life-affirming ways of living together?

I find the standard answers in the forms of 'let's get back to normal,' or, alternatively, 'let's start doing the right things' shallow and misleading. They are wolves in sheep's clothing: new attempts to put ourselves back to sleep. After decades of work listening to human beings, I conclude that in this moment we human beings must develop new, vigorous, and at the same time more subtle ways to navigate in these volatile worlds.

I have long maintained that it is nearly impossible to do anything of lasting importance by oneself. You will find here utterances that have come from my mouth, or have come off the ends of my fingers at the keyboard. More importantly, however, is that what I have said has emerged from conversations with colleagues, clients, family, friends and mentors. The publication of the collection of essays that begins with this volume stems from the work of a group of talented people who have joined me in an endeavor of love, commitment, and mutual respect.

Laurie Dent used to say she was sad that most of the work I have done has been visible only in the midst of programs costing millions of dollars and taking years to yield their results. Hopefully this exercise will change that.

In the essays sometimes names have been changed to protect identities but I have not attempted to bring the essays up to date. The concerns to which the essays are directed are for the most part timeless.

Chauncey Bell

Seattle, September 30th, 2020

Acknowledgments

My thanks to those responsible for bringing these essays together:

- Saqib Rasool has been my trusted advisor and business partner for many years.

- Andy McBride has been my *aide de camp* and partner in the design of these books.

- Margaret McIntyre has been my favorite editor for more than a decade, making sure that I made as few stupidities as possible and that what I say is intelligible. She has been invaluable as a partner in thinking how to express what I have been struggling with for so many years.

- Victoria Ruelas, collaborating with Saqib, originally helped to envision this collection and has led the design and production of its volumes.

- Michele Gazzolo is helping me invent the form and face of what we are doing.

- My wife Shirah, my daughter Livia, and my son Stefan have made important contributions to these volumes.

Finally, I extend thanks to my most important mentors: my mother and father of blessed memory; my wives and children; Fernando Flores Labra, who for 40 years has been my friend, teacher and collaborator; and Joseph, my dear friend for decades, who helps me keep my sanity.

I am grateful for the gentle wisdom of William Butler Yeats in this fragment from *A Prayer for My Daughter:*

Considering that, all hatred driven hence,

The soul recovers radical innocence

And learns at last that it is self-delighting,

Self-appeasing, self-affrighting,

And that its own sweet will is Heaven's will;

[We] can, though every face should scowl

And every windy quarter howl

Or every bellows burst, be happy still.

Contents

Chapter 1: Chauncey Bell?

My intention with these first three chapters is to show something about how my skills and sensibilities were constructed – how this person was invented. For readers who have ambitions to navigate effectively in the middle of ongoing changes or to bring new worlds, this background is deeply relevant. Building a self with particular commitments and capabilities is an important point of departure. At the same time, I am not interested in just telling my personal history; this is not a memoir.

As diagnostician, designer, and implementer of new ways for people to observe the worlds around them, I have been immersed in many enterprises, industries and cultures. On occasion I have taken roles as an executive responsible for ongoing development or operations, which have placed me at the center of political and organizational storms. Today I work as an independent business consultant in an extended network of consultants, designers, researchers, technologists and academics.

Early in life, I began learning to hold onto big questions, allowing these questions to mature, evolve and shift into adjacent questions, grow into bigger questions and stay present over long periods of time. By big questions, I mean questions about how things come to be, what effect they have in our lives, why they stick in our lives, and how to bring new things and effects into being. I credit my parents for infecting me with what we might call 'curiosity.' I don't have a good interpretation about how they did that or how I have held on to it. However, I do think that the gift is much more important than the word 'curiosity' conveys.

One of my first big questions arose when I was 12. I asked myself and my mother why my father did not have time to play with me. After a bit of the kind of investigation that a 12-year-old can do, I grasped that his excuse had to do with something he called 'work.' So, I asked myself, "What the heck is this thing called work that was a sufficient reason for him not to spend time with me?" That question has stayed with me for decades. It grew and morphed into adjacent questions, as I investigated management, leadership, government, education and other related topics. I have been reckless, sometimes courageous, and steadfastly committed in following a number of pioneers of the first order as they asked potent questions such as this and developed new paths for answering those questions.

A formidably important feature of holding on to big questions is avoiding the temptation to put more attention on answers than on the space for inquiry that questions open. I like to joke that when asked questions, Americans regularly make a terrible mistake. What mistake? We answer the questions! And in the moment that the answers appear the listeners get satisfied and the questions disappear. Of course, Americans are not the only ones who make this mistake!

In this chapter, I introduce myself to provide context for the questions I have been living in for many years. These experiences and others have led to the essays later in this and upcoming volumes.

Early Years

My first serious job put me squarely into the middle of big questions. While completing an undergraduate degree at Harvard College I needed more money than my parents were able to provide.

A friend found me a job interviewing and doing library research in the Business Research Group at Arthur D. Little, Inc. (ADL). At ADL, I supported the work of their consultants and conducted the first of the many thousands of interviews I have done since. To my surprise, when I graduated, ADL hired me as the youngest member of the professional staff of the group that had spawned The Boston Consulting Group and Bain & Co.

During my years with ADL, I witnessed the emergence of the current era of public education, printing, publishing and the computer industry through engagements with leading enterprises in those fields. I began to track questions that accompanied these developments, including how products are conceived and designed, and how market positions are defined.

One of my most interesting engagements started when a senior colleague asked me to read and report on the case notes for a large engagement for RCA's computer division. He had fallen behind and I was to help him catch up. RCA had asked ADL how they could get to 10% of the computer industry – the minimum share that their board had decided could sustain them in that industry. At the time, they were one of several firms trailing far behind IBM. As the work proceeded, I was asked to lead our conversations with RCA about our casework, supported by a large team that included several very senior computer scientists.

By extending existing market analyses with speculations and then testing the results (I called it a parametric analysis) I discovered that in one part of RCA's product line they had already reached 30% of the market, despite the sophisticated predatory practices that IBM used to squash its competitors. The staff at RCA had not pierced into the standard industry reports that showed lower market shares. When I reported this conclusion in a meeting with 20 or 30 executives and their staff, I stopped my presentation and watched as one of the senior staffers leaned over the shoulder of RCA Executive Vice President, Chase Morsey, and whispered in his ear. Morsey raised his hand and asked what was our source for that conclusion; his staff, he said, assured him that there was no data to support that anywhere. I told him what we had done and watched as he turned around in his seat and told his assistant to be quiet, listen, and learn. In the same presentation, we told them that we were recommending that they copy IBM's programmatic interface so that programs written for IBM computers could run on RCA computers. Originally our team had explained to me how that could not be done. After serious arguments, our team and RCA's people discovered that this was actually possible. As it turned out, that turned out to be the strategy that allowed Amdahl to become a strong competitor to IBM.

After watching my presentation, Chase Morsey sent a headhunter to recruit me away from ADL. I accepted the position of chief of strategy for RCA's computer division, reporting to Ed Donegan, the CEO of that division. I left ADL and prepared to move my family from Boston to New Jersey. At that moment, RCA's board hired a new CFO for the computer division. He demanded that I report to him, not to the CEO, and that my initial salary be reduced. The salary I had been offered "did not fit his ladder." I told the CEO that I could not start our relationship with them after they had just broken their first promise to me. I had quit my new job before leaving for New Jersey. The complexity of corporate politics, I was to learn, was no less subtle or hairy than the politics of local government. As time went on, I found that I was pleased with the instincts that had told me that the breaking of a big promise would have profound effects on how we would be able to work with each other.

Even though I had taken a risk by walking away from this big opportunity, I ended up being unemployed only a day or two. A close friend came looking for me and asked me to help him develop a program to address the weaknesses and corruption in the criminal justice system in Boston. Fred Scribner, a well-known lawyer from a political family, had just finished helping write the "Safe Streets Act." His mission was to guide the city in bringing federal funds to address the messes there. I joined the Office of the Mayor of Boston as deputy director of the Office of Justice Administration. With this position, I began nearly a decade in public service. I hired a staff, learned to dance in a political bureaucracy, and began to engage with questions of power, corruption and criminal justice. In the world of Mayor Kevin White, I learned to navigate in a "machine democratic city government" administration. The infamous councilwoman, Louise Day Hicks, spoke out against "Chauncey Bell and his gang of unemployed intellectuals!" As we secured federal grants to hire people into the cash-strapped mayor's office, the patronage secretary (a key figure in a machine democratic administration) and I became close allies. She would find people to work for me who at the same time would work on their off hours in projects for the Mayor. I scratched her back and she scratched mine.

After a couple years, I left the mayor's office to work with the US Conference of Mayors and the National League of Cities on a project with the mayors and chiefs of police of the 50 largest US cities as they grappled with the messes of civil disobedience, management and corruption in their criminal justice systems in an era that had important similarities to what we are currently seeing in the US in the Covid era.

All of this brought me face to face with kinds of power that I had only imagined or read about. People in our criminal justice systems deal with and are authorized to exercise physical violence. The moods and sensibilities of the people dealing with those matters on a daily basis are outside the experience of the vast majority of us. Some of the people I met in the criminal justice systems in the largest cities in our country were among the wisest and kindest people I have ever known; others were emotionally closed or damaged by the constant tensions, institutional resignation and having to confront situations in the margins of our worlds every day.

After these assignments, I moved to San Francisco with my family and started my own consulting firm. Initially my clients were police departments, but shortly I moved on to projects concerned with the behaviors of people in city governments. Among other things, I sold, designed and supervised projects implementing early distributed computer systems to address political and operational challenges.

For Kevin White in Boston, we built a system that tracked the requests that came to him from the moment they arrived in the "Little City Halls" to the moment they had been completed. He wanted to know where in the city government the best work was being done so that he could direct more of the government's work to his most effective people. Looking back later, I would see that I was continuing a serious and practical investigation into the question of how people coordinate action when they are working in the world.

For the Secretary of the U.S. Department of Housing and Urban Development, we built a system that tracked all her correspondence with constituents. Too frequently in her meetings with the Congress, a congressperson would begin with a criticism that her department had not responded to some difficulty that a constituent had complained about. When we completed our work, if the Secretary was attacked in congressional meetings about the department's failure to address particular constituents' complaints, the computer-supported system allowed her to answer directly questions about what she had done with the complaints of a particular constituent and then move the conversation back to the department's work program, budget, or other topics in which she was interested.

During this time, I had my attention on the urgent concerns of my clients. At the same time, I had not forgotten my opening questions about what we human beings are doing when we are 'working.' Navigating in the midst of political and bureaucratic enterprises with the concern of bringing changes is challenging, especially as our Western commercial and political cultures tend to be well-defended against change. Curiously, instead of finding myself terminally frustrated and resigned as were many of the people I encountered, I found myself energized by the challenges. I took the challenges as invitations to think and extend my questioning and learning.

I was even more inspired when I heard from a friend who had worked with me in the Mayor's Office in Boston. He posed this question: "What could be done to improve the management of state and local governments in the US?" I said I thought it was a good question, and that I bet if he were to ask that question to professors at business schools, he would get dozens of different answers. My friend, George Kuper, now the staff director for a national commission studying productivity in the US told me they had come to the same conclusion: the question had not been well framed or examined. He asked if I would contribute to the work of the management committee of the commission. I accepted his offer and for the next couple of years, I spent much of my time reading the literature of management and interviewing business school professors with a team working out of San Francisco.

During this time, respected voices in the field of management spoke optimistically of the imminent arrival of "the science of management." Business schools and schools of public administration were dominated by discussions about "decision-making." Today the descendants of those voices are dominated by optimistic conversations about data, evidence, and AI. By the time I had finished my work with the national commission, I had concluded that most of us talking about management knew close to nothing about what was really going on when people said they were managing!

At the same moment, I spotted an anomaly. In contrast to the claims about management science, decision-making, choosing among alternatives and the like, Stafford Beer, the cybernetician, said that the heart of management was to be found in human communication. Beer's idiosyncratic books The Brain of the Firm (1972) and Platform for Change (1975) were written during and after his involvement in something that is becoming better known today as Project Cybersyn in Chile. I was convinced that Beer was onto something that the major figures in popular and academic management circles had no idea about. To my surprise, very soon Beer's work would surface in my world, far more than as ideas and sentences in two books, but as relationships and a path to a different future. In a few years I would come face to face with the man who had designed the work Beer had done in Chile.

Chasing Anomalies

Anomalies – all but invisible elements of our current realities that anticipate and invite different futures – are fundamental for building new futures. Back then, I called them 'weirdnesses.' As an example, today's global Internet began as communications protocols and systems used by my father's colleagues to conduct conversations among the U.S. Department of Defense and a few universities. Most of us had no idea that the DARPANet even existed. It was a "weirdness.".

On finishing my work with the national commission, I turned my attention to some weird stuff: unconventional explorations of what we understand is going on as people are working together. Depositing my last report to the national commission in the main SF post office, I walked up California Street to the offices of EST, an Educational Corporation, and asked to be enrolled in the next offering of their training.

By this time some hundreds of thousands of people had participated in the ever-controversial EST training[1]. During the two weekends of the training, I was fascinated by their interpretations about how we human beings think about ourselves, our worlds, and each other. I loved the way the trainers and people in the EST organization exposed and untangled narratives of personal victimization that surround us everywhere. I had long since concluded that most of us in the West are immersed in narratives in which we explain to each other how we are victimized by our circumstances.

On the night before the second weekend of the training began, my back went into spasms. When I was 12 years old, x-rays had revealed that sometime around the age of six I had crushed three lumbar vertebrae. Every year thereafter, I spent several weeks completely incapacitated on my back with intense muscle spasms. Typically, these episodes began when I did something stupid physically. This time, however, the episode came out of the blue, with no trigger that I could see. My wife asked me if she should call the EST organization and warn them that I would not be coming. I told her that I suspected that the episode was being triggered by the experience of the training, and asked her to ask if I could do the second weekend on my back on the floor of the training room. They said "come on in!" By the end of Saturday's session, I discovered new things about the pain in my back. Pain, it turns out, is as much a function of memory and the way neurotransmitters in the body communicate pain as it is a function of the physical damage to some part of the body. By Saturday evening I was up, walking and out of pain. That was the first time one of those episodes had ended in less than several weeks.

---

[1] https://en.wikipedia.org/wiki/Werner_Erhard

A month or so later, a new acquaintance invited me to suggest improvements to the management practices of an EST trainer named Laurel Scheaf. He told me that she was managing a team of 400 volunteers who were responsible for putting on the Erhard Foundation Physics Conferences[2]. It was an interesting challenge. Later I realized that these conferences were making an important contribution to the world of academic physics. I had already discovered that something about the way that the organization managed its volunteer programs was distinctive and effective. After interviewing him, I offered a sketch of how she might consider organizing the work of her 400 volunteers.

I was invited to attend the meeting in which my friend would be presenting my suggestions to Laurel and 15 women who were her deputies in managing the team. I sat at the back of the room of 25 people who were there for their regular meeting. I listened to his presentation. He used the sketch I had given him. When he was finished speaking, Laurel thanked him and then she looked in my direction and said, "Chauncey, could you add anything to what Bruce has said?"

I was surprised because I had no idea she even knew who I was or that I was present in the audience. Bruce had not mentioned me in his presentation. Obviously, she had done her homework and figured out that I had been involved in his work. I offered a few comments. When I finished speaking, she asked if I could stay after the meeting to speak with her.

As the meeting progressed, I watched admiringly at what this woman was doing with her "volunteers." By this time, I had a great deal of experience with the way that many highly trained, talented, widely-respected managers and leaders worked in a large number of commercial, political, and military organizations. Yet, I had never seen

---

[2]http://www.wernererhardfoundation.org/physics.html\#:: text=For\%20ten\%20years\%20othe\%20Werner,leading\%20thinkers\%20in\%20the\%20field.

anything like what she was doing. She was interacting with each of her deputies as a coach, speaking strongly and directly in front of their peers about what they were doing well and badly. Her people were eating it up! I watched as every member of the group listened intently to what she said to them and to their peers. They moved seriously to adjust themselves to her suggestions, requests, orders, inquiries, and invitations. It was wonderful. How the hell did she do that?

At the end of the meeting, we sat together and she told me that Werner Erhard had asked her to find someone to understudy her role as the leader of this team. She asked if I would be willing to take that on. It was an irresistible invitation. I accepted, and for the following months I spent more time with Laurel as an unpaid volunteer than with my consulting practice or with my wife.

Working with Laurel, I learned more about this remarkable woman. After a few weeks, she introduced me to Erhard. I was invited to various events and dinners at his home, and led a long presentation with him about the upcoming Physics Conference. After a while it became clear to me that Laurel had been preparing me to join Werner's staff.Later, I accepted an invitation to do just that.

When the moment for the Physics Conference finally arrived, the conference participants – a dozen or so of the finest physicists of their time from all over the world – would meet each day in Erhard's office on the top floor of his brownstone home and office in San Francisco. In this logistically complicated event, the 400 volunteers did all manner of jobs ranging from chauffeuring the participants and acting as secretaries, preparing and staffing the spaces involved in the event, preparing and serving meals, and much more. As the conference was about to begin, the manager of Erhard's office, one of the EST trainers, was indisposed, and I was asked to run the house while the Conference was underway. Managing his house was a famously difficult job. However, I knew the house staff, the 400 and their managers, the protocols, the designs, and what was supposed to happen. I agreed, on condition that I would be replaced at the conclusion of the conference in a week or 10 days.

As it turned out, I served in that role for 18 months. The job was similar to running a small exclusive hotel with regular small conferences and meetings, a five-star restaurant with a new menu every night, one dining room table seating anywhere from 6-10, and one or two permanent occupants. I worked roughly 18 hours a day, 7 days a week for that whole period. Finding a replacement turned out to be more easily said than done. Erhard was a demanding boss. He and I would pass in the hallways in the small hours of the morning. With a smile he would warn me not to attempt to keep up with him. It was physically and emotionally the most demanding job I had ever had. Each day began when the chef went to the market at around 5am to purchase food for the day, and proceeded through setups for meetings, meals, dinner, and events. It ended when the chef and his assistants finished cleaning up after the evening's events, usually well after midnight. The chef would nap during the day. I had to verify the progress of everything during the day. The world around Werner Erhard had a shocking capacity to go haywire just when everything looked like it was going swimmingly. The house had a permanent staff of about 10, and on any given day some dozens of volunteers would join in the work.

One particularly interesting aspect was learning about the effect that running on 3-4 hours of sleep for months on end had on my mood and intellectual capacity. I managed to maintain a balanced positive mood, and never stopped finding the challenges fascinating. In some moment, however, I noticed that as I actually approached working 20 hours every day (meaning that my sleep was approaching 2 hours a day) I found myself in what I called 'a fugue state.' I began having trouble telling the difference between what I was seeing and what I was dreaming. One day I remembered a lovely dream about meeting and being invited to have dinner in New York with James Levine, the Music Director of the Metropolitan Opera. The dream made me happy and I reflected on it from day to day. A week or so later I was going through the book that I carried in which I kept track of all my appointments, contacts, promises, and the organization of the work of "the house," and I found Levine's address and phone number. It had not been a dream! He had been at dinner with Erhard and others one evening, and had invited me to come have dinner with him. In my fugue state I had transformed an actual event into a dream. Finally, I left the job of managing the house.

Fernando Flores

My present understanding of myself as a diagnostician and designer began nearly 40 years ago when I met Fernando Flores Labra. A friend called me one day and urged me to meet with Flores, who had been a minister in the Chilean government of Salvador Allende. Following a stint as a political prisoner after the military coup, Flores had been released to the US after interventions by Amnesty International, Stanford University, and other officials. He was working in Stanford's computer lab while completing a PhD at Berkeley and Stanford. My friend mentioned a paper that Flores had written that he was sure I would be interested in.

I found the paper but it was impenetrable. I called a friend and asked him to help me make sense of the thing. In my living room, we read out loud to each other the paper's 58 paragraphs. For each paragraph, we summarized in a single sentence what we thought the author was saying. Then we read our 58 sentences aloud to each other. Reaching the end, I spoke my amazement: "He has cut the Gordian knot for the field of management!" He had found a way to approach the question of what we are doing when we are working that rendered the constraints in the traditional understanding moot.

I arranged to meet with Flores. As we sat talking on the steps of my office in SF, I said "I understand you are from Chile." He nodded. I asked if he was familiar with the work that Stafford Beer had conducted during the Allende regime. "Yes," he said, "I invited Stafford to come to Chile to do that work, and he did his work there on my project." I was stunned. At that moment I said to myself, "This is the guy who had the big questions that I had attributed to Beer," and I committed never to let him get away from me. My journey had brought me back to the center of the questioning that had started when I was 12 years old, about what is happening when we are "working."

Fernando was completing his PhD thesis. and I began to meet frequently and spend long hours in conversation. He introduced me to the work of Martin Heidegger, Hubert Dreyfus, Terry Winograd, John Searle and John L. Austin, in whose company he was thinking. Heidegger and Dreyfus were leading figures in Continental Philosophy, concerned with the questions of "how being comes to be in the world." Winograd was at the time a former enfant terrible in the new field of artificial intelligence and had become a professor of computer science at Stanford. His students there were to go on to found enterprises such as Google and LinkedIn. Searle and Austin were major figures in the world of the Analytical Philosophy of Language who were concerned with questions around how we make things happen in language. Flores had his work cut out for him with his new student Chauncey Bell.

Late in 1981, I became Flores' chief of staff, focused on launching several new initiatives. Shortly thereafter, Flores acted as a matchmaker, bringing Alice Kaplan and me together, and before long we were husband and wife. The picture is from our wedding, with Flores, my best man, in the background, and my wife and I in the foreground.

The next decades were packed with fresh starts, successes, mistakes and failures, contingencies and turns of fortune. We founded Action Technologies, Inc. and Logonet, a training company. In addition to staffing Flores, I had the role of designing The Coordinator™ Software, and was subsequently appointed President of Action Technologies, Inc. I was fortunate to work with a team of brilliant computer scientists from Mexico led by Juan Ludlow Saldivar and Raul Medina Mora, and James Gosling, author of Java™.

Early in the life of Action Technologies, we licensed and connected a network of over 100,000 Coordinator users, and were granted patents for several inventions for coordinating human action in digital networks. Long before the Internet appeared and came into general use, we licensed our software to connect large networks of microcomputers to Novell, Inc., which used the software to connect their Local Area Networks across the planet. We also licensed IBM to use our designs for coordinating action in digital networks.

A few years later Flores conceived a three-year-long educational offering he called "The Ontological Design Course." Over the following decade, close to 750 people participated in 'the ODC.' After nearly a decade of offering educational programs, in 1989 Flores founded Business Design Associates and I was named Vice President for Design.

The most widely published example of the work we did at BDA happened after we taught Cementos Mexicanos (CEMEX) to deliver concrete on time in Mexico City and Guadalajara. While working on other matters for CEMEX, we encountered a world in which mistrustful (and intelligent) Mexican customers of ready-mix concrete, delivered in those big trucks with rotating balls on the back of them, had a standard practice of ordering two loads of concrete and then cancelling one as the day wore on. What was going on?

The concrete was relatively expensive and the companies delivering it were uniformly unreliable in their deliveries. Heavy traffic in Mexican cities was a reliable excuse for tardiness and unreliability. When the concrete arrived on site, a crew needed to be ready for it, because once mixed in the truck the concrete would harden in less than two hours. So, someone would repeatedly call both suppliers asking how soon the load would arrive, decide which supplier was the bigger liar, and then cancel that order. Of course, by that time usually both orders were already on the way, so the driver of the truck carrying the cancelled order would have a problem. The expensive steel ball on the back of his truck would shortly have hardened concrete inside it! At that time the sides of the roads in major Mexican cities were frequently littered with concrete that had been hastily dumped from trucks and with the steel balls from trucks whose drivers had not been quick enough to dispose of their loads. The project was written up in the Wall Street Journal and other magazines, andbooks were written citing that work. For some years, many consultants in the US and Europe carried articles about our work often citing it as an example of "out-of-the-box thinking."

Over the years we built other practices for Cemex, including new mergers and acquisitions, and investment management processes. Cemex went from being a regional Mexican cement company to the third largest in the world and second largest in the United States. Over the roughly 8 years that it operated, BDA built new practices for major companies in the US, Latin America, and Europe. At peak it was a $50 million/year firm employing 75 people.

Matthew Hancocks , my friend and former business partner, focused his Philosophy PhD at Essex University on the development of consultative practices in the West in the last decades. His thesis recognized the work that Flores,I and our colleagues had done. I greatly appreciate his interpretation about our work:

> *Flores, Bell, and their colleagues were fired up by the insights brought by an understanding of human being as an emergent form born of history, biology and language as emancipatory*

and creative. They invented coaching and consulting practices and taught themselves and their clients to see themselves not as victims but as subjects for invention of futures. They developed structures to allow themselves to master promises for the future. They built exercises for making cool assessments and delivering direct, sometimes even harsh assessments. They worked on themselves to cultivate moods that would allow serenity in the face of contingency. In short, they taught themselves and their clients to turn their language, their historicity, and their bodies into technologies and to design themselves to become disclosers of better worlds. Their thinking and practices were ahead of their time and at the same time absolutely of their time. They were pioneers creating the world that came about.

They did not see fully the degree to which they were wielding a double-edged sword. They were actors on the developing world stage. Not the dominant actors – McKinsey, BCG, and the Monitor Group would take those roles in the field of consulting – but actors nevertheless. Many others copied parts of what they were doing.

Today we cannot avoid following threads from the games that BDA designed to our present circumstances. Their designs included a compelling call to strive for exceptional results, a relentless focus on designing and reifying our embodied reactions, language actions and sense of self, and a focus on financialised metrics for performance. Today we witness a world led largely by ultra-rich and agile achievers hurtling without sufficient narratives, maps, or compasses towards an unknown future.

At the turn of the millennium, Flores left for Chile where he was elected Senator and served for 8 years. As he departed, he licensed BDA's intellectual properties to VISION Consulting, S.A., an Irish company. As a consultant to VISION, I served as group director and designer for work in England, Scotland, Ireland, Germany, Switzerland and the US. At the conclusion of his term, Flores returned to the US, and we reconnected and resumed our collaborations.

Over the years of working with Flores, I came to focus on questions about what human beings are, how we invent our worlds and futures, what technology is and does, and what money and finance are all about. I now understand myself as a designer and intervenor in what I call messes – situations that communities of intelligent and well-meaning people find themselves in after years or decades of adjusting behaviors and processes without deep understanding of who we are and how we live in language.

Seattle

After 35 years in the San Francisco Bay Area, in 2007 my wife and I moved to Seattle so I could take a senior role in a new company, CareCyte. We intended to bring facilities for the next generation of healthcare. About a year earlier, an architect friend had asked me to look at how he and his colleagues were attempting to improve the way that hospitals were being built. I agreed. He introduced me to the way that they were using 'Lean' methods in planning and construction. I had close experience with the work of Taiichi Ohno (the engineer who had invented the Toyota Production System). The 'Lean' discourse is an American interpretation of tips and techniques from what Ohno did, built from Western business academic and journalistic traditions. I looked at the work going on in the hospital construction industry that my friend was involved in. It was clear to me that they were "looking for love in all the wrong places." What American and European imitators of Ohno's work had failed to introduce into the automobile industry, where it had been invented and was so desperately and obviously needed, would certainly fail to produce the desired transformation in the healthcare construction industry.

The first paper that I brought to my friend was titled "You Can Waste a Lot Looking for Waste." I explained that to fix the hospital construction business, the 'Lean' proponents were attempting to use a set of practices that the Japanese had invented and attempted to bring to the American automobile industry starting in the 1960s. My friend George Kuper, the man who asked me to help with research on improving the management of state and local governments for the national commission, had been one of the American Automobile Industry executives invited by Toyota to visit Japan as they were first sharing the Toyota Production System with the Americans. He reported the following comment from the US delegation's cocktail party conversation at the end of their first day in Japan. "How stupid do these people think we are, trying to convince us that they can run an automobile manufacturing plant without inventories?"

Not only did the US automobile industry skim tips and techniques from what Toyota offered us. We, the US, failed utterly to learn what we had been offered. Over the following 50 years Toyota went on to become the dominant player in the global automobile industry. Finally, in 2008, only the intervention of the US government actually saved Chrysler, Ford, and General Motors from bankruptcy.

There are tremendously valuable insights available in the Lean discourse as it exists in the West. However, it is not the universal panacea that its devotees have sometimes found themselves compelled to claim. US management discourses are not simply resistant to innovation and change; they are arranged in ways that protect them from the very orientations and moods in which learning and rapid progress takes place. As I have said before, we learn to ride bicycles by falling off them. Our managerial and business education practices develop ways of listening, posturing, leading, and managing that don't allow the kinds of behaviors and orientations in which rapid and serious learning thrives. Speaking into that background, those enamored with the Lean tradition have often found themselves compelled to take strident positions claiming far more for their methods than those methods deserve.

So back to CareCyte. My Seattle-based business partners included a distinguished hospital architect, several doctors, and an engineer who had been responsible for the structural engineering and design of perhaps a quarter of the tall buildings in Seattle, along with Paul Allen's extraordinary Experience Music Project (now known as the Museum of Pop Culture). We brought an investment banker from New York to help us. My colleagues had conceived an approach to building modular hospitals composed entirely of steel and polymers that could be adjusted over time to fit the changing requirements of health care practices. At that time over 5,000 hospitals in the US were over 50 years old, prohibitively expensive to renovate, and full of bugs (the microorganisms that lead to "nosocomial" – hospital-born infections) that could not be eliminated because of the style of construction in which they had been built. Our steel and polymer designs offered vastly lower costs, shorter lead times for the construction and expansion of such spaces, and bug-free environments for modern medicine. We envisioned a generation of immaculate, state of the art hospitals suited for the kind of medicine arriving right now, improving the quality of healthcare and access to it. However, it was not to be. 2007 was a bad time to start such a venture, and we made several important errors. After three years, concluding that we had failed, I returned to my traditional consulting practice, and my wife and I elected to remain in Seattle.

Arriving in the Present Moment

My business is building practices. For five decades I've worked with people and their enterprises as they learned to break old habits and build new ones, liberate themselves from traps and open paths to new futures. I've designed and led projects bringing major innovations to industries ranging from computers, digital networks and semiconductors to wholesale and retail banking, utilities and finance, heavy equipment manufacturing and in the public sector. In each project, I was helping communities build new practices and new worlds.

Among the oft-cited stalking horses of management, leadership, and innovation, the practice of building new practices has not yet emerged as distinct. On the face of it, this capability – mobilizing new ways of working – sounds simple. It is not. Imagine keeping a house together while taking it apart to rebuild it for new purposes. The skills involved in building new practices are likely to become essential capabilities in the century we have recently entered. No textbook yet embraces this puzzle: you cannot build new practices without simultaneously performing at high levels of competence in the more common skills of managing, leading and innovating. And those skills do not themselves reliably yield new practices or intentionally-shaped new worlds.

One way of saying what this first volume is about is that it is my serious, nay impassioned, invitation to join me in the exploration and articulation of what we need to develop on our way to a deeper understanding of how we human beings can build new practices for ourselves.

Chapter 2: Preparing to Dance

Give me a place to stand, and a lever long enough, and I will move the world.

> – Archimedes

Theory without practice Is empty; practice without theory is blind.

> – Harold Anthony Lloyd

In our normal common sense, to make sense of some world we must appropriate an awesome range of 'information' about everything in that world. We must study and become acquainted with a vast array of disciplines, occupations, businesses, technologies, the literature and the traditions inhabiting it before it will be possible to make good sense of what is going on there. In that interpretation, the job of working with people to make their worlds more habitable, flexible and understandable, and then to partner with them as they adapt themselves to changing circumstances is more than voluminous; it is impossible. In that interpretation, one can learn about, make sense of, and make a difference in only a tiny range of worlds. Facing this impossibility, the vast majority of journeyman consultants, professionals and advisors who attempt to work with different businesses and industries retreat into specialization, methodologies, tips and techniques, rules and the like. They proceed on the basis of their experiences and intuitions, and as a result, are largely ungrounded.

Instead, the foundation of observing ourselves in action upon which I have built have allowed me to be effective in a wide variety of different worlds. To that end, this chapter dives into the challenge of constructing a unified place to stand from which it is possible to make sense of and effectively interact systematically with many worlds.

Biology, History, and Language

Fernando Flores introduced me to the interpretation that we human beings are constituted in biology, history, and language, intertwined in ways that hide what is going on.

First, we are biological organisms, dependent upon our bodies for everything that matters to us and the way that those bodies belong to our physical worlds and the earth. Our biological dimension includes many things, beginning with what we call awareness or consciousness, the continuous force of gravity, the air we breathe, the cellular structures and water that comprise all of it. Our dependence also extends to the condition of the planet.

Secondly, we are historical beings, constructing our ways of thinking about ourselves and our worlds from our experiences and our understanding of the pasts we inherit, the present moments of surprise, boredom, awe, what we call memories, and the futures that we dream and commit ourselves to produce.

Thirdly, we are linguistic beings, the kinds of beings who live in distinctive ways in language. Here I do *not* speak of language merely as particular constructions of words and sentences, but as a name for the space in which we listen, dream, fall in love, speak, act, and interpret everything about ourselves and our worlds. The philosopher Martin Heidegger tells us we are the kinds of beings that live in language.

We are also the kinds of beings who construct various observers in our conversations, including the three I have named here, thereby allowing ourselves to invent and examine interpretations of ourselves and our worlds. Fernando Flores was for me a fourth observer, critical to bringing me to watch the other three perspectives.

I remember watching him explore these phenomena shortly after we began to work together. One day he was trying to make sense of the emotions and moods in which we encounter each other, build relationships and trust, and organize action together. On this particular day, he was thinking about the 'moods' of different animals – especially dogs and cats – as they meandered and acted in their worlds. He spoke about what we could call the taken-for-granted predispositions and preparation for action that postures gave evidence of – the cat watching and getting ready to pounce, or the dog standing its ground and warning nearby animals not to mess with it. Dogs and cats don't get to cultivate their moods. Their postures come with their biologies. We human beings have the privilege of observing and commenting upon our emotional states. We cultivate new sensibilities and skills that help us as we navigate in our worlds.

In the nearly 40 years in which I have had the extraordinary privilege of dancing with Fernando Flores, I have been grateful for many things that have come from our interactions. Fernando built his insights from his life experiences in his home country, Chile, with his family and his networks, and from his study, readings, and interactions with the many teachers, colleagues, and giants on whose shoulders he stands. He shapes his interpretations with care and patience. He has brought to those of us who have been able to study and work with him a host of teachers and collaborators, living and dead, who speak to us across time.

Taking Language Seriously

The senior of the three phenomena in which we constitute ourselves as human beings is language. Everything that exists (and can be referred to) in our worlds exists because we have observed, conceived, found its name or named it in language.

Words and sentences are obvious but language, the space in which we discover ourselves, is mysterious. Notwithstanding the sheer ubiquity of language, it is slippery and often misleading. Encountering language as more than the simple exchange of words is not typical in our modern world. Learning to listen to ourselves in language takes time and courage. Language always stands ready by our side to teach us in speech, writing, dreams, poetry, and action. At the same time, language does not hesitate to hide itself and ourselves from us. It appears to lend itself to conceptual manipulation as do, for example, Arabic numbers. Countless partners in marriage and business say to each other every day, "I heard what you said," as if that was as obvious a truth as '2+2=4' without grasping that very often we completely miss 'what was said' in the background, between the lines, or in the mood of the exchange. In the moment that each of our utterances appears to open and clarify some aspect of life, language is busy hiding other matters from our attention.

Action and Language

The idea that when we speak, we commit to something is very old. At its root, it points to the recognition that speaking and creation are deeply connected. In translation to English, Bereshit, the first book of the Torah, begins with a passage that says:

*When God began to create heaven and earth— the earth being
unformed and void, with darkness over the surface of the deep
and a wind from God sweeping over the water— God said,
"Let there be light"; and there was light.*

In the Christian Bible this appears in the Gospel of John 1:1:

*In the beginning was the Word, and the Word was with God,
and the Word was God.*

The British philosopher John Langshaw Austin is widely credited
with calling attention to what he called "performative" verbs. These
verbs animate all modern languages. In the tradition of Austin, his
pupil John Searle and his student Fernando Flores, I have come to
understand performatives as verbs that 'do things.' When I promise
to finish this chapter, I am not merely describing what I intend to do;
I am committing myself to an action. Or as Fernando mischievously
used to say, "You're fired" is not information; if the speaker has the
authority to say that, the saying of it changes your world.

Readers often get tangled up in the difficult language of Austin's work
and the distinctively geeky appearance to modern Western eyes of the
person of John L. Austin – an Oxford Don. These can tempt us to
dismiss his work, but we should recognize that he was the man who
organized and managed all Western military intelligence leading up
to the Allied D-Day invasion. Austin was a profoundly practical
man: a superb investigator and keen interpreter of what was really
going on in his world. In my view, this blend is magical: practical
and operational skills and a deep understanding of what is going on
when those skills are being exercised. (My father, Chauncey Bell Jr.,
of blessed memory, had some of the same characteristics.)[3] The fact

---

[3] For the last 20 years of his working career, he managed Aircraft Maintenance Logistics Studies
for the U.S. Air Force at the Rand Corporation. He kept 3,000 planes flying. I miss him.

that Austin did all this work – what happens as we are speaking and listening to each other in language – in the middle of the greatest of our wars, and in the middle of the biggest mess of allmakes it all the more remarkable.

Fernando Flores encountered Austin's work through conversations with Austin's student John Searle, one of Flores' thesis advisors. Flores recognized that performative verbs comprise the heart of every action and everything that matters in all of our worlds. Up to that moment, Austin and Searle's work had been understood as "Speech Act Theory" – a subject of great interest to a tiny population of academics studying the analytical philosophy of language in a half a dozen graduate schools of philosophy in the world. To Flores, their thinking showed itself as something of enormous import for our modern world. Here is my summary of what he grasped:

> *We invent all of our ventures and enterprises with declarations. We make offers which, when accepted, become our promises to customers, investors, employees, and friends, family, and others. Everything that is new begins with assessments we make about insufficiencies, messes, opportunities and obsolescences. Our enterprises are created as networks of requests, offers, and promises. Everything else that happens starts with requests and offers. We make sense of ourselves and our worlds through assessments and assertions. Money lives in the middle of all this as a collection of commitments, often in hidden and secret ways.*

In bringing the work of Austin and Searle to our interpretation of life and commerce – what we do together in the world – Flores invited us to build a new language for understanding a world which had previously been understood as *decisions, doing things, making profits,* and scores of other names that describe things and completely miss the point of how we do things with words[4]. In cleaving open this field, he invoked a new space for design, action and diagnosis of the difficulties, messes and mysteries in the world of people at work and in life.

Flores invited the world to create a new "clearing" (a phenomenon we introduce in the next section) and invent new narratives to open a space for interpreting what we see, what matters and what we care about. Many of his clients and students have credited Flores with producing radical changes in their lives and worlds. The effect is not accidental. From his first encounter with the work of Dreyfus, Heidegger, and Austin, Flores understood something profoundly important about human beings and language: that with performative verbs, we invent and change our worlds.

Power and the Clearing

Years ago, Fernando introduced me to what he called "the clearing." He told me that if I began to understand the working of the clearing, I would find it much easier to understand and interact with the backgrounds of those I was guiding, teaching, counseling and coaching. I listened carefully, and after some consideration, said I did not believe him. It seemed to me, I countered, that he wanted to convince me that my very challenging work was going to be easier if I were to study something that sounded like a fantasy, some metaphysical nonsense. He responded in a way that was, in my experience of him, unusual. He said, "OK; then consider what I am saying and see what you see over the next several months, and then come back and tell me what you think." It did not take months. A few weeks later, I went back and told him that I was convinced that there was

---

[4] Austin, J.L., How to do things with Words, Harvard University Press; 2nd Edition (September 1, 1975)

something happening in the background that could not be explained without something like what he called "clearings." Since that time, I have repeatedly been stunned by the power of the all-but invisible phenomenon of "clearings" as they shape what people listen, how we think and react, and what we say and do.

Yuval Noah Harari, Seth Godin, and others refer to this phenomenon as "narratives." Tamim Ansary calls them "constellations." Here is a recent speculation from Godin hinting at the power of the phenomenon:

> *If we give an isolated community access to the internet, very quickly, the quality of life will improve. Time will be saved, research into proven solutions will produce value, and people will become connected to a larger population. Those connections will lead to productivity and learning.*
>
> *And, then, soon thereafter, they will become less happy.*
>
> *Not because they're worse off, but because the dominant media narratives that arrive exist to make them feel insufficient, inadequate or simply jealous at how green the grass is over there. Our narrative defeats our surroundings, every time.*[5]

The splendid Hubert Dreyfus, standing on the shoulders of his teacher Martin Heidegger, said this about the phenomenon:

> *Put generally, the shared practices into which we are socialized provide a background understanding of what counts as things, what counts as human beings and what it makes sense to do, on the basis of which we can direct our actions towards particular things and people. Thus, the understanding of being creates what Heidegger calls a clearing (Lichtung) in which things*

---

[5] https://seths.blog/2019/10/narratives-about-modernity/

and people can be encountered. Heidegger calls the unnoticed way that the clearing both limits and opens up what can show up and what can be done, its 'unobtrusive governance (Waltens).'

For Heidegger, the history of being in the West has been the history of misunderstandings of the clearing. From the Pre-Socratics on, philosophers have sensed that something beyond ordinary being was as responsible for their existence as anything, but since the clearing, like the illumination in a room, must always stay in the background–or, as Heidegger puts it, withdraw––to do its job of letting things show us, philosophers since Plato have replaced the clearing with a highest being that is the ground of beings and the source of their intelligibility. For Plato the highest being was The Good, for Aristotle, The Unmoved Mover, for the Christians, The Creator God, and, after the Enlightenment, it was man himself. Heidegger calls all these attempts to replace the clearing with a 'beingest being' onto-theology. ... [A]ccording to Foucault, power has suffered a parallel misunderstanding.[6]

What I am calling 'the clearing' has appeared as an invisible governor defining what matters, what exists, what needs and does not need attention, and is busy feeding interpretations to everyone in every work experience I have ever had in public and private sectors.

I propose that one of the most important jobs for those of us who care about our communities, families, and worlds is preparing the space for observing what clearings do and building new narratives and clearings to begin to displace current, obsolete, misleading, sometimes obscene clearings and narratives. Without addressing these unseen governors, the task of addressing the messes in our worlds is

---

[6] Hubert L. Dreyfus, "Being and Power Revisited" in Foucault and Heidegger: Critical Encounters, edited by Alan Milchman and Alan Rosenberg

continuously misleading or too often pure waste. We will need to cultivate and shape new narratives and practices with the love and care we are sometimes able to give to raising infants of all species.

Maps to Bring Human Conversation to Center Stage

In every domain of recurrent human action, we make maps to help us have efficient conversations with each other – about where we are traveling, about how we are going to lay out the kitchen for preparing our meals, about the schematics of the semiconductors we are building, about the layout of the new bathroom, house, office building, or mall. There have been many attempts to map the territory in which I work where, in conversations with each other, we invent our futures and worlds. We have organization charts that illustrate hierarchies of authority and power. GANTT and PERT charts show the flows of actions of various kinds of things. Biological and genealogical maps illustrate our inheritance of genes and genetic predispositions. None of these traditions began from the place where this story needs to begin: in the way we human beings invent our worlds in language.

In his PhD thesis, Fernando began with an exploration of several traditions for understanding management. In that background, he invented a design for a machine he called "The Coordinator" to help actors in organizations get oriented, bring forth linguistic actions to start other actions, and keep track of the commitments that they and those they were collaborating with were making with each other. The thesis described how 'customers' and 'performers' bring action through conversations that begin with requests or offers, proceed through negotiations to promises and shared commitments to build new conditions of satisfaction, deliver those new conditions of satisfaction, and finally complete with the customer declaring his or her satisfaction with what was produced.

In the early-1980s, Fernando brought Juan Ludlow and James Gosling, talented computer scientists, to San Francisco to develop the first prototype of the device he had envisioned. James, the lead computer scientist involved, was beautifully prepared for the work. He had previously built the highly regarded Gosling Emacs Unix editor, and was later known as the father of the Java programming language.

Flores asked me to collaborate with them and to help turn their work into a product. They were thinking from state diagrams included in his thesis that described 'the conversation for action.' The proposition of the thesis was compelling to all of us. As we began to explore the capacity of early versions of the prototype to allow us to conduct conversations through the device, we discovered a daunting difficulty. The initial characterization of the unity of a conversation for action was clear, compelling and complete. In practice, however, as we conduct conversations of any richness or complexity, we bring in new elements for clarification, context, digressions, recollections, references, and other matters. The human nervous system does not have difficulty keeping track of these conversational elements, but computer systems of that time did. Keeping track of conversations within conversations inside a data processing device gave us fits. We could see that the tool we were engaged in building was going to be inordinately clumsy to use.

Juan, James and I had a long conversation exploring this, and then I had a conversation with one of the philosophers helping us with our work at that time. I concluded that to have the coordinator work we would need to declare a rule to the effect that the machine would deal only with one 'primary' conversation at a time. Any and all subordinate conversations and conversational fragments would be organized 'around' the primary conversation. In the moment that the primary conversation no longer functioned properly as an organizing focal point, then that conversation would need to be closed and another primary conversation opened.

We went on to develop two successful generations of The Coordinator. At first, we deployed it in an extended network of about 100,000 people – mostly entrepreneurs and small businesses using it to help them coordinate action with each other. In the years of its global operation, we never heard a complaint that it had lost track of a single conversation or misinterpreted what was going on in those conversations. Eventually we licensed the communications capability of the software to Novell where they used it to connect their local area networks around the globe. Finally, as we turned our attention to other opportunities, we stopped supporting the coordination software.

This was the beginning of the series of events that led to my inventing something that we would soon begin to call 'the loop.' The loop, a simple drawing of an ellipse divided into four quadrants and charting Fernando Flores' *Conversation for Action*, has become an essential component in a graphical language that we have invented for mapping the actions that human beings do as we coordinate our actions in conversation with each other.

The next significant event in the invention of the loop occurred when people from IBM approached us and asked us to explain to them what we had invented out of Flores' thesis and in the construction of the early coordinators. They invited us to present our findings to senior staff members from four IBM laboratories studying processes. The IBMers were convinced, in advance, that there was no possibility that we could have invented anything original. They had been working on the question of processes for many years. However, they were willing to listen. Fernando, Terry Winograd and I decided that we needed better graphics for talking to the IBM experts about what we had been inventing, and so Fernando hired a graphic design firm to help us with the construction of our presentation.

The graphic designers sat with me as I described what we had invented, listening and exploring what kind of graphical representation we might use. At some moment in the conversation, one of the designers, looking at the way that I was moving my hands as I was describing what we had invented, said, "Why don't we use what you are doing with your hands as the central image?" I had been moving my hands in elliptical patterns as I described the dance of the conversation for action, which ended where it began, with the completion of the action opening a new space for thinking, invention, and action. The path I was tracing was the path of a helix, the two-dimensional aspect of which is an ellipse. We built our presentation for IBM around this new diagram for the conversation for action, a loop with four quadrants.

The loop maps the journey we take in the most fundamental actions of coordination that we human beings do with each other. We travel the loop hundreds of billions of times each day, beginning with requests and offers, in every language known to mankind, in every nation and community on earth.

UNIVERSAL CONVERSATION FOR ACTION
(The Unity of Service)

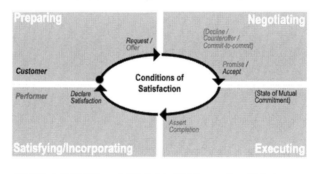

· The conversation for action begins at 9 o'clock with listening and preparing, with assessments about things that are missing, broken or in the way, and leaps into life on arriving at 12 o'clock. There, the arrowhead represents the moment when a customer makes a request or a performer makes an offer calling for a new future condition of satisfaction.

· From 12 o'clock to 3 o'clock the conversation for action is about negotiation by the parties, exploration of the consequences, investments, counter-offers or a decline of the offer or request. The successful next action following a request is a promise. If the conversation proceeds from an offer and the offer is accepted, that becomes a promise. So, if the conversation is successful and is proceeding with a promise at the arrowhead at 3 o'clock, the parties arrive at a mutual commitment to deliver a particular future condition of satisfaction. They have a 'deal.'

· From 3 o'clock, the performer in the conversation goes to work to produce the actions necessary to deliver the agreed-upon conditions of satisfaction, and at 6 o'clock the performer reports what has been produced.

· From 6 o'clock, the customer reflects on what has been produced, incorporating the new condition of satisfaction into his or her world, or declines to accept what has been delivered as being inconsistent with what had been requested or promised. If accepted, at 9 o'clock the customer declares themselves satisfied with a 'thank you.'

The IBM process researchers declared that what we had invented was in fact original, and asked for a license to use what we had invented. They paid a great deal of money for it!

Over the following months and years, we built a language and set of graphical devices for producing maps showing the way that the action in human enterprise is enacted in conversations among the people in those enterprises. As a shorthand for what we will spend time exploring in a later volume in this series, the following characterizes important structures in the graphical language we invented.

Commitment Process Maps in a Nutshell

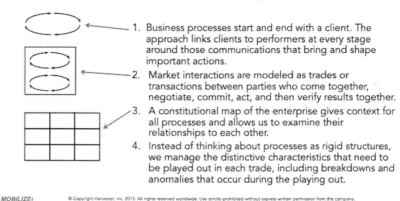

1. Business processes start and end with a client. The approach links clients to performers at every stage around those communications that bring and shape important actions.

2. Market interactions are modeled as trades or transactions between parties who come together, negotiate, commit, act, and then verify results together.

3. A constitutional map of the enterprise gives context for all processes and allows us to examine their relationships to each other.

4. Instead of thinking about processes as rigid structures, we manage the distinctive characteristics that need to be played out in each trade, including breakdowns and anomalies that occur during the playing out.

Applying the method and mapping practice reveals:

· What each party has committed to do.

· How work is delivered when we do it well.

· How to diagnose what goes wrong.

· Where we have dissatisfied clients and why.

· How to improve the way we work.

· When we have lost trust, and how to rebuild it.

· Where we are responsible (and not).

· Where we are competent (and not).

Two of the most important applications of this new language are 1) diagnosing the messes that come from historic habits of speaking and listening in communities, and 2) preparing the space for building bridges to alternative futures.

In this case diagnosing means answering three questions. First, what is the situation in which a community finds itself? And what explicit and implicit conversational practices are shaping the way that the community deals with its world and its challenges? Second, how did the community arrive in this situation? Third, why and in what way is the community unable to move to a new situation, to escape from the trap of its current situation even though the community has many capable, mature, responsible people in its midst.

Until the moment in which this new language and practice of mapping coordination appeared, this dimension of human experience – the coordination of action in language – had not received formal attention from the right map-makers. Over the years since what I described here, I and others who have worked with us have learned that working with the loop reveals miraculous things about how we human beings invent our futures in language. This is how we make the future happen: speaking and listening in conversations with each other.

An Exercise in Observing our Worlds

Once we grant to ourselves a richer, greatly expanded understanding of what is going on as we are speaking and listening, the notion that we invent our worlds and futures in language appears simple, all but obvious. Over the years, however, I have discovered that it is actually quite obscure. As I have endeavored to train younger consultants, I would ask where they thought things came from, and the answers were almost always more or less like the naive Lean syllogism "if you ask why 5 times, you will get to the root cause." This is absolute nonsense. Not that there's anything wrong with asking why repeatedly. That's a good practice. The nonsense is there is no such thing in human experience as a root cause. In physics and chemistry, sometimes, yes. If you mix hydrogen, oxygen, and a spark, you will get an explosion and water. In human interactions, never. Complicated biological, neurological, historical and other factors underlie the intrinsic conversational and intellectual laziness we all embody. We settle very fast for answers about why things are happening, where they come from, and what keeps them in place in our worlds.

The exercise that follows is designed to awaken our raw sensibility to where our worlds come from. The exercise is best done with a partner, but you can do it alone. It is extremely simple. Print out the following prompts – questions you will ask yourself during the exercise – and then take a walk in your neighborhood. As you walk, follow the prompts that appear below, asking each question in your conversation with a friend, or talking to yourself as you walk and observe what you find in your neighborhood.

1. Yourself

· What is your name, and where did it come from? Who named you, and in what traditions did they name you?

· What are you wearing, and where did the clothing come from? Who defined the articles of clothing you are wearing, who branded them, and who taught you to wear those clothes?

· In what way do you think about the kind of person you are, and from what traditions and what speakers do you take the discourse about the kind of person you are?

2. **Town or city**

· What is the name of the jurisdiction in which you are walking, and who gave it that name, when, and in what tradition?

· What are the boundaries of the jurisdiction? Who defined those boundaries, and when?

· In what style or political tradition is the jurisdiction governed, and what recent changes are appearing in the rules and habits of behavior in the jurisdiction?

3. **Roads and paths**

· How did these get here? Who asked for them, who paid for them, who designed them, who installed and who maintains them?

· What are the traditions of driving and walking in the jurisdiction? Right or left side of the road? What about the signage? What kinds of rules prevail? Traffic lights? Stop signs? What are the consequences of following or not following the traffic instructions embodied in the signs?

· Do people in this jurisdiction follow instructions or not?

4. **Conventions**

   · Do strangers greet each other when they pass? Smile at each other?

   · How close to each other do people stand when they are talking?

   · How are others dressed?

   · Who picks up the litter? Do you stop and pick up litter?

5. **Homes**

   · Are the homes in the neighborhood well- or ill-kept?

   · How are the boundaries of properties marked? Are numbers visible on homes?

   · What rooms are located on the public sides of the homes? Kitchens? Living rooms? Why? Who put those rooms there?

6. **Woodlands**

   · What are the names of the trees and plants you see there? Do you know some of those names? Who gave them those names? Where would you go to find out what their names are and what is the history of naming and thinking about those names?

   · Who put those trees and plants there? In what kind of conversation did they define what would be there, and how they would be arranged?

   · Who cares for the trees and plants? Why?

7. Enterprises

· Are the names of companies displayed on buildings? Why? Why not?

· Why are there people in those buildings?

· How did they get there, really – not that they walked or drove – what language-actions led to their being there?

8. The Sky

· Glance at the sky.

· How many features of the sky can you name? Where did those features get their names?

· Why are those features important? Why do their names 'stick'?

9. The Earth

· Feel the earth under your feet.

· What sensation does it give you? What do you call that sensation?

· Where did you learn to call the sensation what you called it?

10. Divinities

· As you have walked and observed, have you experienced the emotions we call 'gratitude' or 'awe'?

· How did you express those emotions – to yourself privately or out loud?

· Do you refer directly to the divinities ("the gods" or God) or do you avoid speaking in that way?

Now walk back to your home and explore what shows up as you read and reflect on the few sentences below.

1. The terrain you are exploring is local and familiar; we are not asking you to figure out stuff that does not belong to your own neighborhood. There is enough 'data' in the background of our normal everyday common senses so that you can bring pretty rich conversations about how a particular fireplug happened to arrive at a particular spot without having to undertake a major research project.

2. The exercise opens the opportunity to reflect on the connection between the way that the world of artifacts – things in our worlds – intersects with our customs, laws, and historical conversations.

3. The exercise enriches an already existing narrative that we share with others about what is already in our everyday world in a way that allows a rich conversation and the possibility of glimpsing something transcendent.

Like it or not, paying attention or not, each day we participate in shaping our worlds. Most of the time we participate in ways that are innocuous, harmless, and to which we are asleep, ignorant, or blind. We go along with what is happening. Sometimes we are thrilled by something: a sunset, the smile of a child, wonderful weather, magnificent music, a well-prepared meal. Displeasure is more common, and it is far easier to make a negative assessment than to acknowledge something that contributes to us. We complain to ourselves or to those around us, or to the gods. "It should not be this way!" "Why doesn't someone do something about this?!"

Some of us will set out to deliberately and passionately take responsibility for (and brave the risks) that are involved in bringing new futures. We can learn to pay attention to the moments in which we glimpse and then confront phenomena and situations that are unhealthy for us, or that suggest new possibilities and openings for us. In those moments sometimes we can encounter ourselves as people who are being offered the gift of participating in the creation of important features of our worlds.

And sometimes in the moment that some of us are granted those opportunities we are actually aware of what is happening – that new worlds are being disclosed in our conversations!

In my experience, this exercise can dramatically increase our capacity to observe the world being invented and reinvented around us every day, and to appreciate the capacity we have as human beings to participate in the creation of our worlds.

Chapter 3: In Conversation with Chauncey

For years I have said things in provocative ways. Those who know me and have worked with me will recognize this as a pattern in my conversations. I look for ways to 'pull the rug' and land us on our proverbial behinds. My provocations are designed to allow us to confront conventional wisdom that we have taken for granted and to give us the opportunity to scratch our heads and say, "I wonder if there is actually a different way of thinking about this situation." The structures that I called Five Great Wastes, Nine Principles for Navigating in Our World and my essay Wise Organizations? are examples that can be found in this and the following volumes.

I have been thinking about the provocations I introduce here for some time. I intended them to unsettle interpretations that most of us take for granted without any awareness of how they tangle our thinking. I'm interested in upsetting interpretations that, for the most part, live in the background of our awareness. Those interpretations tranquilize us. They encourage us to stop looking for answers to what appear otherwise to be relatively unimportant questions. They tell us not to waste our time worrying about such matters. Without our even noticing, our conventional wisdom has convinced us that we don't need to challenge ourselves to look further. It doesn't even occur to us to question our assumptions.

There are many provocations I could write about, but I've chosen seven as examples to get us started. They point to fundamental assumptions about the way things are. These provocations should help us get started questioning what we take for granted.

- Listening

- The Conviction that Thinking Happens in Our Brains

- Overestimating the Value of "Intelligence"

- Compumorphizing

- The Perceptual Faith

- Victimization

- Questions of the Gods

Listening

The part of language that we can watch – speaking – dominates our thinking about language. Our common sense treats listening as secondary and passive. Long before there is any action, however, before there is any thinking about actions that might be taken, we are listening without realizing that we are doing just that. Listening to the situation. Listening to each other's interpretations of the situation. Listening (and not listening) to our own moods and emotions. Before we notice it, listening is already shaping the possibilities for action that will show up later.

The central and longest essay in this volume explores listening. When our business is bringing new human practices, listening must get a new, central role. Listening, especially listening to what we have not listened to before, and what we have avoided listening to because it repels us, is going to get increasingly important in this world as change accelerates all around us.

We take for granted that listening is something that we turn on and off at will. On the contrary, we are listening all the time, awake or asleep, sensible (i.e., 'conscious' in our common understanding) or insensible, paying attention or not. We are always listening – to noise, to silence, to music, to poetry, to our experience, to our dreams, to each other, to the way we are not listening to each other, to what is happening in our bodies and our nervous systems, to our moods, to the moods of others around us and on and on. The question "What is going on when we are listening?" has served me as a huge space for observing human beings–the kinds of beings we are, our concerns, our habitual ways of interacting with each other, and what we are oblivious to in many different ways.

Everyone is listening all the time, whether aware of it or not. Listening is receptive, whereas speaking is assertive. Speaking is planting and listening is gathering and harvesting. Listening is quiet, while speaking is noisy. What would it be like to walk around the earth just listening, not speaking?

Even though we are always listening, we aren't in charge of how we listen. Before we enter into conversation with someone, we are already listening in a particular way. Many listening techniques instruct us to become a blank slate. Here is the bad news: even at the moment of birth, we were already listening in a particular way. We are not open, impartial, empty vessels, able to begin from a blank slate, nor are we able to stand reliably in each others' shoes. We are structurally-determined biological systems[7] listening within structures originally laid in place literally millennia ago.

---

[7] From Humberto Maturana and Francisco Varela, Chilean biologists and friends of Fernando who became dissatisfied with a biology that could make no sense of language and cognition except as metaphysical phenomena. They invented another biology with which we can understand language and cognition as biological phenomena. This is a topic for another moment.

We acquire our listening from our historical, inherited ways of interpreting the world – historical discourses that we embody from family, geographic location, gender, our prior experiences, and the historical events in which we have lived. Originally, we all absorb these ways of interpreting uncritically, not noticing that they produce a particular way of interpreting the world. We assume our way of listening shows us 'reality,' the 'truth.'

We go about our lives deeply involved in our day-to-day activities, only rarely stopping to consider whether what is obvious to us is obvious to others. It is only when we are able (or forced) to step back and observe our lives that we can even notice our listening.

In important ways, I think of listening as the first question of being human. We were listening from inside our mothers' wombs before we were born. In our early years when everything was new, we were immersed in our listening to everything. We only learned to begin to claim that 'we already knew that' after a few years of being alive. Very few philosophers have taken the question of listening seriously. Listening is not part of the essential training of physicians or of many other occupations where listening is fundamental to performance.

Listening happens biologically, historically, and linguistically, as we will explore in the listening essay later in this volume. For the most part, listening is unmapped territory. Until a couple of millennia ago, the geographical world was unmapped. Before the 18th and 19thcenturies, human biology was unmapped. Technological computation was unmapped before the 20th century. The coronavirus was unmapped before our current time.

Why is this important? Because all kinds of mistakes, miscoordinations, and horrors begin in unmapped territories. Unmapped territories abound with lore, legends, theories, literature, hopes, dreams and lurking monsters. Though it is fundamentally unmapped, listening dwells with us continuously, in a myriad of ways. It is, in my mind, the beginning of everything in life. When we pay attention, our listening continuously presents surprising possibilities.

As a point of entry to this conversation about listening, I recommend taking a stand on listening: declare yourself ignorant and a beginner in the world of listening, or at a minimum, declare yourself to be without an adequate set of distinctions for navigating reliably in the world of listening. Commit yourself to attend to the phenomena and to learn about it. Commit yourself to a predisposition in which you make yourself available to have your way of knowing, your thoughts, and your emotions interrupted and altered by the process of listening to others. Usually, to risk less is not to listen.

The Conviction that Thinking Happens in Our Brains

Our current thinking about thinking can be traced back to Rene Descartes (1596-1650). We use his name to label our tradition of treasuring the kind of thinking we call rational. We call it Cartesian. Descartes said "Cogito ergo sum: I think; therefore I am."

We live in the conventional wisdom that thinking happens in our brains. This conviction leads to all kinds of difficulties and silliness. For example, we compete with each other, criticize, complain, and ridicule each other for our respective intelligence. We struggle to maintain trusting relationships with each other. And all the while, if we look closely at what is going on when 'thinking' is happening, we can see that in the vast majority of cases, when important thinking is actually happening, it is happening in our conversations.

Yes, we each have a brain, but when the job is more than rendering memories of facts and thinking that has already been completed – more than making assertions about facts and the truth of matters – most of the time the crucial work happens in conversations among two or more people.

Overestimating the Value of Intelligence

One of the important names we have for our inborn, ready-to-hand capacity to navigate in the world is intelligence. Sophisticated moderns know that the whole capacity with which we navigate in the world lives not only in our brains but in our nervous system as a whole, and at least to some degree in the cultural systems provided by our worlds for moving around in the world. The process of walking, for one basic example, is guided by the interactions of nerves and musculature in our legs and hips; recent research undertaken at Carnegie Mellon University where they were studying how to control robots walking has shown that the brain gets involved in walking only when obstacles such as steps are in our way.

We find no difficulty with the idea that what we call intelligence guides us in selecting particular actions, and avoiding others. There is, however, a problem with this interpretation. It is undeniably true that in doing common everyday actions – those with which we are intimately familiar through life's experiences – we depend upon the capacity of the embodied intelligence born of our experience. That is how we find our way to the bathroom, brush our teeth, crack the eggs we are going to cook for breakfast, and regulate the heat under the pan as we cook the eggs.

When we encounter situations unfamiliar to us, however, the intelligence born of our experience is missing things. In small ways, this happens to us more or less daily. When we enter a situation that is unfamiliar to us, we start needing to depend upon counsel from others. The old joke about the problem of men not asking for directions gives a hint of where I am headed.

I have spent a lot of time thinking about this, particularly in the context of working in large enterprises and in the world of modern healthcare. In both of those worlds, we are in trouble when we encounter a situation in which the combination of our experience and the vast trove of information available to us through our smartphones and computers don't deliver effective or trustworthy recommendations about what path to follow. In those moments, we make assessments that tell us *whose* assessments – judgments about how to move in the situation – we will trust and follow. I claim that this particular capacity – of making assessments about other people's capacity to make assessments – is even more important than our overall general intelligence. Think about it.

The genius who has difficulty establishing trusting relationships with other human beings is in trouble. He will not be able to commit to follow the counsel of some advisors and to discard the counsel of other advisors.. Recently I experienced a cardio-neurological event – a stroke. While I was hospitalized and examined with a CT scan and other fancy imaging, I learned that the neurologists caring for me had extraordinarily good practices for what to do in the moment of the stroke, and, sadly, not a clue about where the stroke had really come from. Worse, on leaving the hospital, I discovered that they were hopeless about how to avoid a subsequent stroke. On careful examination, I found that their counsel followed lines that were designed to protect them from future litigation for not having given the orthodox recommendations. They left me on my own to sort out what to do next.

I wrote on the whiteboard in my office a list of the dozen physicians of various sorts with whom I was exploring the circumstances of my "event." The list included two cardiologists, some neurologists, my primary care physician, a practitioner of Chinese medicine, a dear friend trained as an engineer who had practiced as an emergency room physician for 30 years, my daughter-in-law who is a professor of nursing, a homeopath, a naturopath, two dentists, and even a veterinarian friend. I was clear about which of those physicians' advice

I was following, and which physicians' advice I was going to listen to but definitely not follow. If I had gone higgledy-piggledy back and forth among those advisors trying to find out whose advice worked best for each feature of the experience of the stroke, I'd have been in deep trouble. Initially I discarded all the neurologists from the list, and then eventually I did find a neurologist whose advice I could follow. She had had a neurological event herself, had undergone brain surgery, and was wise to the difficulties of her field. Eventually I put my primary care physician, my Chinese medicine physician, and my friend with the emergency room experience to the top of my list.

The interpretation that I have developed about the importance of the skill of assessing others' capacities to make valuable assessments first emerged 15 years ago while I was watching my son Nicolas struggle with physicians who were attempting to diagnose and guide him after an accident in which he had crushed several vertebrae in his back. While he was following several other young men on bicycles coming down a precipitous path on a mountain in Chile, he missed a turn, went over the side, and landed on his helmeted head 12 feet below the path. Those he was following were locals familiar with the path; he was not. The following day he was in enough pain to be frightened. Some weeks later, back in the U.S. and still in a lot of pain, and still without a solid diagnosis of what was producing the pain in his back, I overheard Nicolas on the phone with a friend, cursing the doctors who "couldn't make up their minds" about what to do about his pain. By then the physicians had said that he had crushed four vertebrae in his upper back. At the same time, this conclusion was spoken by physicians observing images of his spine, not living in the middle of his spine.

Listening to him, I realized that in the mood in which he found himself, he was in real trouble and was not learning how to have effective relationships with his doctors. He thought that they were able to observe directly what was causing his pain and were having trouble getting into action. He did not understand that an x-ray of something is not a simulacrum of the phenomena. It is a device that invites skilled people to make interpretations about what is going on and then, on the basis of their skills in their particular domains of skill, they can make recommendations about courses of action. He needed to shift his interpretation about what was going on. So I began to explore that with him.

In the world of health, allopathic medicine (i.e., traditional Western medicine) is one of the marvels of the modern world. When we seek the care of an allopathic physician in one of the many domains in which they have developed advanced skills and reliable practices, often they are able to produce what would have been considered, only decades before, miracles. A broken arm, even a compound fracture? Appendicitis? Diabetes? (They replaced my left hip this year with titanium, glass, and polyurethane parts in a procedure that they completed, to the point of my waking and talking with them, in one hour.) Extraordinarily clear and reliable interpretations, precise and clearly articulated diagnostic parameters, and procedures to address a wide variety of situations are ready-to-hand.

At the same time, for complicated reasons that we will not go into here, allopathic medicine is also a domain in which there exist enormous territories – whole continents, if you will – of unexplored phenomena. And if you happen to arrive at an allopathic institution with symptoms in one of those territories, you can find yourself in serious trouble. At that moment the crucial skills are the capacity to assess the capacity of other people to make good assessments, and then the capacity to develop trusting relationships with those whose counsel you are going to follow.

Compumorphizing

In March of 2008, Jill Bolte Taylor, a neuroanatomist, gave a TED Talk that she called *My Stroke of Insight*. It was a beautifully delivered report of what she had discovered and concluded following a stroke she had. She brought to the presentation an actual human brain to help drive home the significance of her report. The talk led to an appearance on Oprah, a book, and some fame.

I watched her talk with deep interest and some concern. (Had I been looking at the talk in 2019, after my own stroke, I would have had an even deeper incentive and perspective for paying attention, but that was later.)

On April 2, 2008, I posted a comment in my blog about her talk. After acknowledging the beauty and relevance, I complained that it was misleading in important ways. In that posting I coined the term '*compumorphizing.*' Now, 12 years later, I continue to think that Bolte Taylor's mistake – projecting the structures of computation on our understanding of brains, thinking, and being human – is terribly important. Today, in fact, the practice called Artificial Intelligence is coming into its own with machines challenging or surpassing human 'intelligence' – the capacity to do what we commonly understand as *thinking*. In many fields even the experts are having real difficulties articulating the difference between human beings and machines. And that is not a trivial matter. The casual technological observer today may say that this is not important. I insist that it is.

In my blog post, I said the following:

"Science is about the development of speculations that are then tested with facts that are tested for their truth or falsehood. Taylor's talk is not that. In it, the speculation comes at the end, after a great number of language actions, most of which are not facts.

Friedrich Nietzsche said this about truth:

What, then, is truth? A mobile army of metaphors, metonyms, and anthropomorphisms—in short, a sum of human relations which have been enhanced, transposed, and embellished poetically and rhetorically, and which after long use seem firm, canonical, and obligatory to a people: truths are illusions about which one has forgotten that this is what they are; metaphors which are worn out and without sensuous power; coins which have lost their pictures and now matter only as metal, no longer as coins.

(Quoted from http://www.geocities.com/thenietzschechannel/tls.htm)

"The truth is a mobile army of metaphors." Ms. Taylor has marshaled an army most of whose members sound familiar to us, but I recommend caution. The metaphors belong to the past, not the future, and while her story is touching and passionately spoken, and her concerns deeply worthy, I find her story about where the future will be found deeply flawed. We can learn a lot from examining the metaphors she has chosen as her army for truth, and the kinds of language actions in which she brings her interpretation.

The aspect of the talk that I find most worrisome is the way that Taylor has appropriated a combination of computer and new age distinctions as the core metaphors for framing her interpretation of the human experience. When we say that someone is 'anthropomorphizing' something, we mean that they are taking the human being as the frame for understanding some non-human phenomenon. For example, we say, "the computer wants attention," shorthand for a psychological desire concerning the way that the design of the computer couples with human beings. Is there a way of saying the opposite?

How do we say that someone is using the frame of distinctions that we use to build computers to understand something so non-computerish as a human being? 'Compumorphizing?' That is one of the things that Taylor is doing. I guess that the dangers of anthropomorphizing a computer are not great. When we anthropomorphize other animals, we often find that it is more difficult to do things like training dogs. The downside from interpreting human beings as computer devices, in contrast, I insist, is vast. For one thing, we continue to misunderstand what is happening when people are talking with each other as 'sending messages,' which produces no end of mischief.

I found several parts of the way in which Ms. Taylor constructed her speculation about what human beings are, and what our possibilities are, to be misleading at best or even worse, wrong-headed.

1. In many ways she refers to the way that we 'process information.' Maturana and Varela insisted that brains do not process information, and that there was no way to construct a grounded interpretation of the human being as a concernful autopoetic entity with that distinction. They convinced me, and I am committed to follow their lead in that department.

2. She compares the two halves of the brain as 'parallel' and 'serial' processors. As poetry, this is compelling, but I am pretty sure that this is metaphor, not an actual description.

3. She says that the two halves of the brain are all but unconnected, and shows us the absence of tissue between them. Then she asserts a number of connections between them that, as a number, is simply an abstraction. While physically unimpressive in her presentation of the physical brain, the dimensions, role, and capacity of the corpus callosum that connects the two halves of the brain are more impressive. (From Wikipedia: "The corpus callosum is a structure of the mammalian brain in the longitudinal fissure that connects the left and right cerebral hemispheres. It is the largest white matter structure in the brain, consisting of

200-250 million contralateral axonal projections. It is a wide, flat bundle of axons beneath the cortex. Much of the inter-hemispheric communication in the brain is conducted across the corpus callosum.")

4. She uses the distinctions 'consciousness,' 'mind,' 'energy,' and 'life force power of the universe' without introducing or ground-ing what she is talking about. Each then convokes a domain of metaphor, and while unmistakably poetic, each is also unmis-takably ambiguous.

5. She uses the bicameral brain that she shows us as her portal to talking about 'the we inside of me.'

Like most of us moderns, Ms. Taylor is blind to the phenomena of language and the way that human beings invent our worlds in lan-guage. Listening to her presentation, in moments I was convinced that I was watching a kind of scientific nihilism – a new way of un-derstanding ourselves as the central and only salient elements of the universe. On the other hand, the talk fits some Eastern traditions of thinking about the universe as everything and nothing at once. Ms. Taylor's world collapses to a conversation between two halves of the brain, one of which has been damaged, and suddenly that bicameral unity is all that is needed to understand the entire construction of the universe.

Humberto Maturana and Francisco Varela were inspired by the chal-lenge of making sense of this kind of narrative to develop a grounded narrative about a biology that comprehends cognition and language. I understand that the vast majority of the world has yet to encounter their work, and (like Ms. Taylor) is still using Newtonian biology. Nevertheless, they did develop a new biology, and some of us studied it, and it is available for understanding the kind of phenomena Ms. Taylor is interested in. Fernando Flores was inspired by the horrific results of bad interpretations of what a human being is to bring together the work of Austin, Searle, Maturana, Varela, Heidegger and others into a unified way of understanding the human phenomenon as biological, linguistic, and historical, in which the human being invents concerns, possible futures, actions, institutions, and coping practices in language. Some of us worked hard to develop some competence in this interpretation.

I fear that this talk will become a kind of popular 'muzak' with the role of keeping us asleep about the big question that Ms. Taylor ends with: the construction of the human being and the human experience. It fits with too much of the old story about what animates us, and is missing too much of what I am sure needs to be brought to the conversation if we are to develop a rich interpretation that will support the challenges we are facing in the era we have entered.

Certainly, we must honor Ms. Taylor's courage and give thanks to God, modern medicine, and the people who helped her make her recovery from the blow she was dealt. At the same time, let us be careful not to get lost in the thrall of the enthusiastic crowd. Compelling though the experience of listening to this talk may be, I do not think that it is particularly good news for you and me."

That was the end of my post.

The last three provocations – The Conviction that Thinking Happens in Our Brains, Overestimating the Value of Intelligence, and Compumorphizing – all deal with features of human brains, cognition, and how we think about these. Merlin Donald explores the physiology of the brain and how we understand it in his book, A Mind So Rare: The Evolution of Human Consciousness.[8] This passage from his text can help us understand how some of the misconceptions and confusions have come about.

---

[8] W. W. Norton & Company, Inc. New York, 2001, page 324

The human brain is the only brain in the biosphere whose potential cannot be realized on its own. It needs to become part of a network before its design features can be expressed. Since we are living beings, the networks we create are complex, fuzzy, and multilayered, rather than lean and mean, or driven solely by the needs of symbolic communication. This makes our networks radically different from those that have been invented for nonliving entities, such as computers. The cognitive infrastructure of human culture includes many things that we do not normally call symbolic, such as patterns of public action, the built environment, and conventional expressions of emotion. ... We depend heavily on culture for our development as conscious beings. And by exploiting this connection to the full, we have outdistanced our mammalian ancestors. ... We have lived comfortably with the myth of the isolated mind throughout most of our history. We like to think of ourselves as self-complete little monads dwelling inside our sealed biological containers, peering out at the world from the safe haven of consciousness.

The Perceptual Faith

The philosopher Maurice Merleau-Ponty coined the phrase, "perceptual faith." In his last book, The Visible and the Invisible, assembled after his death by his editor Claude Lefort, he says:

We see the things themselves, the world is what we see...

And then he says this:

> [F]ormulae of this kind express a faith common to the natural man and the philosopher. The moment he opens his eyes [he is relying upon] a deep-seated set of mute 'opinions' implicated in our lives. ... This is the way things are and nobody can do anything about it. It is at the same time true that the world is what we see and that, nonetheless, we must learn to see it.

If we consider carefully what happens in the all-important events in our lives – our conversations in which we learn, think, conclude, and bring action – we will see that the vast majority of what happens in our conversations is actually, and fully, invisible. Consider, for example, the following elements of our conversations. What do we really know about each of them?

1. Language itself (not the words and sentences, but the space from which we bring the words and sentences)

2. Our concerns

3. Emotions and moods

4. Listening

5. Value and waste

6. Commitment and action

7. Learning, sensibilities, and wisdom

8. Money, power, and capital

9. Worlds, clearings, and time

Yes, on first inspection we might say that we actually can see and hear some elements. Take language, for example. We hear words. If it is written language, we see sentences and paragraphs. But what we are observing and hearing is actually only some of the outward and visible signs of inward and invisible graces. Language is multidimensional and subtle. With each visible or audible utterance, when we look carefully, we will see that the same utterance hides as much or more than it reveals.

How about emotions and moods? Yes, we see clear outward signs of various emotions and moods in facial expressions and body language. However, a simple trip to any place where actors are working, in videos or in the theatre we will observe that emotions and moods are perplexing, multifarious, and can be faked.

What about money? Surely the coins and bills, and checks and promissory contracts are physically real and can be observed. They are not invisible! Well, certainly the Arabic numerals and dollar, pound, yen and the like signs that we use when we talk about money are visible, as are the coins and bills. However, money, a specialized, universal linguistic domain, is more subtle than that. I call the interpretation of money that assumes that it is a domain of wholly or even primarily physical and observable phenomena "the Scrooge McDuck interpretation of money." When we talk about value and waste (and proceed casually to talk about how we measure each) we are wandering into a territory that is far more subtle that the common sense presents to us.

This insight, this provocation came to me only a few years ago in my long life. I realized with a shock, as an epiphany, that one of the most important struggles of my life was a misunderstanding. For decades I had struggled to talk with clients and friends about things that I had concluded were important but were not obvious to them. I had understood that the difficulty was in explaining difficult things. I was wrong. The difficulty originated in the fact that what I was attempting to show people was fundamentally *invisible*, not difficult. And making those things visible demands the construction of narratives in which the invisible becomes visible.

Victimization

I do not remember when I first realized that I had a serious ambition to address what I'll call 'our victimization.' Many Western human beings habitually understand themselves as victims of our circumstances. Those raised in the United States, like me, however, think of ourselves as heroically independent. We resonate with Frank Sinatra's, "I did it my way." You might say, "*Certainly* I *am not a victim!*" If you look carefully though, I am sure you will see how this common understanding of ourselves as victims has indeed shown up in your own life. In some moments, haven't you said to yourself or to others, "If only...." or "Why didn't I ...." or "That happened because ...."?

We understand our progress in life, our limits, and the outcomes of our efforts in ways that are framed as consequences of events and circumstances mostly not under our own control. We think we have led the lives we have led because we were born to *those* parents, grew up in *that* city and country, attended *those* schools, missed *those* opportunities that others had, were lucky in some cases and unlucky in others, and so forth. Once we begin to look carefully at these situations, we can see that this peculiar 'pre-understanding' operates unobserved in the background at a level and to a degree that is astonishing. We understand ourselves and what happens to us by following the visible and invisible threads of the contingencies of our histories.

Think about it: While we sometimes tell ourselves that we did something of importance by ourselves, we rarely do. And if that happens, if we look carefully, we can see that all too frequently the speaker is wound up in fantasy, hubris, or caught in self-absorption.

We share this unspoken commitment to search for explanations for our circumstances and assign blame with nearly everyone else. I like to say that we are addicted to interpreting the circumstances of our lives as events in which we have powerful understandings of what caused what. We share these habits of thinking, speaking, listening and explaining with those around us who are also busy searching for explanations. We struggle to understand the causality that we assume must underlie what happens to us. And we construct narratives that position us as the effects, not the causes of our destinies. I am told that Sri Nisargadatta Maharaj said: *All that happens is the cause of all that happens. Causes are numberless; the idea of a sole cause is an illusion.*

In every moment that we understand ourselves as the victims of our consequences, we abandon the high ground. Before we even notice these structures, we have already given away the opportunity to understand deeply that we – each and every one of us – have in every moment the opportunity to alter, shape, and invent our paths, our immediate and potentially distant futures. We do this in conversation and collaboration with those we love, those in our communities, and those with whom we share human destinies. Living a life as a predestined tragedy is tragic. Throughout much of my life, I have committed myself to address this structure that I call our victimization.

Every day these two habits that we have inherited from our (Western) clearing damage our capacity to observe what is going on in our worlds, make interpretations about those things that are going on, and build bridges to alternative futures. The habits – seeking explanations of causality in every moment, and assuming that we are victims of those circumstances in which we are seeking explanations – are not going to go away. They will stay with us until the clearing changes. What we can do with them is watch and remember that these mischievous interpretations are always with us, and constantly suggesting, quietly and in our backgrounds, that we look in the wrong direction for understanding ourselves in our worlds.

Roberto Mangabeira Unger utters the opposite interpretation in The Religion of the Future.[9]

Life is the greatest good. With life come surfeit, spontaneity, and surprise: the capacity to see more, make more, and do more than all the social and conceptual regimes in which we move can countenance. In the face of all constraint, the experience of life is an experience of a fecundity and fullness without foreordained limits.

We exceed immeasurably the social and cultural worlds that we build and inhabit. There is always more in us, in each of us individually as well as in all of us collectively, than there is or ever can be in them. There is always more that we have reason to value and power to produce than any of these orders of life, of all of them together, can contain.

The principle that applies to the organization of society and culture applies as well to thought and discourse. No method, no system of procedures of inference and modes of argument, no apparatus of reasoning in any one discipline, or in all disciplines combined, can do justice to our capacities for insight. We can always discover more than our established practices of inquiry can prospectively allow. Vision exceeds method. Method adjusts retrospectively to suit vision.

We are unlimited, or infinite, with respect to the practical and discursive settings of our activity. They are limited, or finite, with regard to us. Our excess over them is what, in a traditional theological vocabulary, we call spirit.

---

[9] Harvard University Press, Cambridge, Massachusetts, 2014

Questions for the Gods

As I said in the introduction, I have asked myself why I have encountered the gifts of my life. Where have they come from? The
horn of plenty has opened for me with many 'lucky' events: the gift
of rich relationships with my parents and those around them; my
wives, children, grandchildren, friends, access and admission to the
astonishing networks of human beings that I find around me; and
the many times I have escaped death and injury by small margins.

The question, of course, is an invitation to speak about gods. Where
in previous eras we would unhesitatingly have spoken about the grace
of God, or the will of the gods, today we speak words like serendip-
ity and synchronicity to avoid risky references to the gods. It is no
longer politically correct to speak of the work of the gods unless we
occupy the role of a religious leader. In the carefully tended secular
conversations of the 21st Century, we must accept that the business
of the gods is either ludicrous or beyond our comprehension. Our
modern clearings are impatient with interpretations in which we attribute power to gods.

As I said earlier, I am sure that one feature of the way that I have
lived my life is the way that I have held on to big questions, allowing
those questions to evolve and shift into adjacent questions, grow into
bigger questions and stay present for me over long periods of time.
By big questions I mean questions about how things come to be, what
effect they have in our lives, why they stick in our lives, and how to
bring new things and effects into being. Philosophers call some of
these *ontological* questions, and contrast them with what they call
ontic questions, which are about the things and effects that we find
around us. I started with the question of what is going on when we
say we are working. Later, I asked how and why I had broken my
back when I was a youngster. As I learned to live with a condition

that could not be repaired, I began to wonder what kind of being I was with a broken back? Much later, I learned that these were important questions, for me and sometimes for others as well.

As I moved through schooling and entered employment in various jobs, these questions morphed into extensions of my earlier questions. What is really going on when we say we are working? Managing? Leading? John Kotter, the emeritus Matsushita professor of leadership at the Harvard Business School, worked for me as a summer intern while studying for his business degree. Later, I followed him as he went on to become a major speaker on these topics. As time passed, with help from wise friends, I moved to questions about the constitution of being and the way that we make, fulfill, and forget our commitments. I added questions about the institutions of engineering and education, the worlds of practices, and how we actually constitute new practices for ourselves.

For observing the way that we sometimes can find and hold on to big questions, I am fond of the story reported by James Gleick about a conversation between the physicist Richard Feynman and his father. Richard's father had his son watch the way that a marble rolled forward and backward in his little red wagon when he pulled the wagon and stopped it. His father told him that what was going on is called momentum and that nobody knows why it happens that way. "The general principle is that things that are moving try to keep on moving, and things that are standing still tend to stand still, unless you push on them hard. ... This tendency is called inertia, but nobody knows why it's true."[10]

For the great majority of my career, I have had the gift of working with these kinds of questions. Laurel Scheaf taught me to observe people at work with a deep appreciation of being and care. Fernando Flores taught me to read and listen to philosophy, to have a deep

---

[10] James Gleick, Genius: The Life and Science of Richard Feynman, p 29

and abiding respect for language, and many other things. Shirah, my wife, introduced me to Mussar, a millennia-old set of Jewish practices for observing human beings, diagnosing the quality of our practices, intervening in them, and building new ones. My mother taught me to build relationships with other human beings that would serve me well in every part of my life.

Chapter 4: Designing

When Fernando Flores left the U.S. to become a Senator in Chile, I started 'The Design Club.' With a few dozen talented colleagues – including James Gosling, inventor of the language Java™ – I convened conversations to advance our understanding of the practices of design. Abridged versions of the following essay, written for our first meeting, have been published by the American Institute of Architects (AIA) and the Association for Computing Machinery (ACM).

My Problem with Design

I was reminded today of the things I find troubling about our modern notions of 'design' and 'designing.' Hundreds of years ago, if one wanted to become a designer, one would first have become a master craftsperson. We learned how to construct distinctive artifacts (and worlds of artifacts) and then we began to innovate in that tradition. To say one was a "designer" without that background would have been ridiculous.

In his book, FAB, Neil Gershenfeld shows us how, starting a long time ago, we began to separate the "manual" work of craftsmanship and the "intellectual" work of design into two threads, and we began, moreover, to ascribe social class differences to the "types" of work.

The manual work was to be done by lower classes, and the "intellectual" work of designing by upper classes. This distinction, I think, is a poor one, and today gives us no end of messes in our world. The following is a reflection I started writing several years ago, about why that is the case.

When someone says they have designed something, what do we understand? In the world at large, after all, 'design' is something pretty simple and universal. To design is an activity – to devise, contrive, intend, indicate, plan, arrange, strategize, scheme, sketch, or the like. Further, we understand designing as relevant in an enormous range of life's circumstances, usually in combination with two other activities: actions to implement 'the design,' and results produced by the implemented design. Put in its simplest form, ideas are translated into actions that in turn produce results. When our actions lead us awry – or don't give the results we want – we have the option of concluding that the flaw was "in the design."

So why do I say I have a problem here? I have a problem because this way of understanding design decomposes an important unity into arrangements of trivial components. If we observe the activities of a designer in action using the commonplace distinctions of today's normal interpretation of design as an arrangement of activities and components, we end up understanding design as something not very interesting. Imagine that we are observing a competent chef preparing a meal. We have our standard understanding of the activities of designing the menu, selecting ingredients, preparing the food, mixing ingredients, cooking, and tasting. If we attempt to understand the chef's design of a meal as a collection of activities, we will miss the essence of the chef and the meal. Ask yourself, what are the essentials of designing a successful career?, a successful party?, a painting by Picasso?, a graphical layout?, or re-arranging the deck chairs on the Titanic so that they are pleasing to the boarding passengers?

Watching a 'designer' put each into place, and writing a story about each, we will find ourselves confused about what made a difference in each case. Thinking and observing from the commonplace interpretation of design, each project is merely someone's arrangement of components according to some logic that made sense to that person at the time of the arrangement.

I will raise several questions about the way we commonly interpret 'design.'

· First, our way of understanding design strips apart components, activities, and contexts. I like simplification, but not this kind of atomistic simplification that destroys the context.

· Second, the commonplace notions of design don't give observers of the design process strong ways of making sense of the object of the designer's attention – what the designer thinks he or she is designing.

· Third, the designer doesn't have a useful way of thinking about who he or she is in the process of design – the role they think they are playing.

· Fourth, I want to question the accountability the designer takes in the invention of whatever he or she is designing.

Let's take them one at a time.

Atomistic Simplification

First, let us examine the way we remove context in the way we understand design and designing. I guess that several hundred years ago, designers didn't have a distinct role. Builders, artists, engineers, doctors, carpenters, goldsmiths, and others designed and implemented, and did not get separated from their inventions. Later in this paper, I'll argue that we need to find ways to repair the way that designers have gotten disconnected from the concerns of the communities in which they design, and from themselves as actors on the world stage, and that their designs have gotten disconnected from the worlds of practices and things in which they participate. I use the word 'concerns' here not in the sense of 'worries' or 'anxieties,' but rather to point to the rich and complex structures of involvement and care that each of us carry in the background.

We moderns think nothing of removing activities and things from their contexts – from the practices and histories in which they were born. We act as if we can understand things and activities in a way that is separate and distinct from the world in which they exist. For example, we forget that a hammer is only sensible as a hammer when we use it for 'nailing' in the world we call 'building,' where we encounter nails, boards, saws that we use to cut board, the sawmill that produces boards, trees from which we produce boards, forests that produce trees, and so forth. (In another context, of course, we can understand a hammer as a weapon, or as a tool for forcing stubborn machinery to move, etc.) Absent its adjacent network of equipment (and the world of ambitions and activities to which they belong), a hammer is a curiosity, perhaps a work of art, an example of an artisan's work, or some piece of historical detritus, but not what we currently understand as a hammer.

In this era, too often we settle for atomistic simplifications in which we lose essential unities. It is not possible to think in a rich way about things and events and the worlds in which they arrive from descriptions of the things (or services) and characterizations of "what they are for." A great chef boils beef thigh bones for many hours to produce the stock that will be the basis of a great soup or sauce; our recipe books claim to imitate the chef's construction with beef bullion cubes. The world of the design as a historical construction disappears when we think that we have understood it adequately as a thing and its purpose – the hammer for hammering nails, the beef bullion cubes to give a beef flavor to the soup.

For the kind of designer that I am attempting to be, and to prepare others to be, this standard way of understanding design – as a combination of a description and purpose – fogs the mind and impedes or stops innovation. The design of anything of significance, of anything that will result in people having new practices and new interpretations of themselves and the world in which we live, or that will help us reshape our world, for better or for worse, does not surrender itself to such an interrogation of its construction and purposes.

What is Designed

Recently a friend – a design engineer exploring the question of design with me – asked me, "Supposing I asked you to design a new one of these?" He held in his hand a plastic fork. I found it a great question to help me lay out some distinctions about what is being designed. I asked him, "Am I to build a duplicate of the fork – what is specified by the object? Or, perhaps I am to build an improved fork – one that will deal with some of the breakdowns of plastic forks? They do, after all, look tacky and tend to break when you try to cut meat with them. Or, am I to design a new thing that takes care of some of the things that a fork takes care of, but in some distinctive new way?" We can look at the history of automobile design to develop this idea.

In the American automobile industry during the 50s, 60s, and 70s, for the most part the main competitors built the same vehicles over and over, changing their outward appearance, and making incremental improvements in the interior and other characteristics. In that world, designing a new device – say a fuel pump – meant, for the most part, designing a 'new' device equivalent to the last one. Perhaps it would attach to the car in a different way, or have a different profile to fit among other parts more conveniently, or it might have some components improved to deal with nagging difficulties of the old ones. 'Design a new fuel pump,' meant to copy the last one with some slight changes in configuration. We'll call this kind of configuration of a thing (or event, etc.) Type I Designing.

In the 1970s Japan woke up to the opportunity of the US automobile market, and decided to enter the market by building cars of 'better quality.' Instead of simply copying things, they began to pay attention to the breakdowns that people encountered while using their automobiles, and to address those breakdowns. They began to make many improvements to automobiles by designing things that did not break in the same way that US cars did, worked more simply, and so forth. We'll call designing things (and events, etc.) to address historic breakdowns Type II Designing.

Finally, there is a kind of designing where designers go all the way back to interacting with people's concerns, and inventing new ways of addressing those concerns. Here are some examples. The Sony Walkman was invented as a way of making 'a personal music space' available to people, and not as a way of reducing breakdowns in tape players or boom boxes. The modern Japanese motorcycle was invented as an exciting, fast, light personal transportation device, and not as a better Harley-Davidson. Fuel injection was invented as a new way of getting fuel into the cylinder, and not as a better carburetor. When designers are dealing with the concerns that underlie some world of things or activities, and where the things or practices they come up with make a break with the traditions in that world, we'll call that Type III Designing.

Up to this point we are talking only about certain functional aspects of design. Aesthetic questions, and questions about how designs create identities also are profoundly important, and aspects of the same logic can be brought to bear. Take the example of putting fins on automobiles in the 1960's and '70's. I will argue that this was a change in a component – Type I Designing – while if we turn our attention to the introduction of the Volkswagen Bug at the same time we can see an invention that addressed other concerns in new ways, just as we can see that in the Toyota Prius – the "hybrid" gas/electric vehicle. These latter inventions are, I think, examples of Type II Designs. There are many features of our society today that we may, in the future, conclude are their own versions of fins – disposable everything, fast foods that are not nourishing and leave us a nation of fat undernourished people, health systems that are managing the wrong risks, the dot-com madness, to name a few.

When you hear someone asking for "thinking outside the box," they are asking for Type II or Type III designs – designs that break with the tradition of doing things as we have done them before.

Who the Designer Is

Everyone acts in ways that can be understood as designing. Some take on design as a profession, and some of them end up designing fundamental new human practices. Many of those that I understand as designers – perhaps most – do not understand themselves as designers. Rather they think of themselves as innovators, entrepreneurs, or simply people who had the fortune to do some things that changed their profession, their company, or their industry. Some designers understand themselves in terms of the things they design, and others understand themselves as actors on the fulcrum of history.

Many years ago I was speaking with a software designer about his then-current passion for computer graphics. I asked him why he was so focused on the graphics, and he answered, "I just like it." I challenged and teased him, insisting, "You're pretending to be shallow, and you are kidding yourself. Graphics are important because they allow us to catch and shape people's attention. Building more skill with graphics will make you a better designer of people." As a shy, Western Canadian, Protestant male, he brushed away the challenge – deflected, not ignored. On the other hand, he went on to design the most important computer language of our time – Java. The deep structure of the designer's involvement in the world of design often is not readily accessible even to brilliant designers themselves. Yet even the best designers are more effective when these relationships are more accessible.

The distinctive character of the designer shapes each design that affects us, and at the same time the designer is shaped by his/her inventions. Successful designs shape those for whom they are designed. The designs alter people's worlds, how they understand those worlds, and the character and possibilities of inhabiting those worlds. Let's take only one example: the most extraordinary invention of our era: networked computers. The Internet, personal computer, word processor, and electronic communication tools of our world have changed who I am (and who each of us are), for better and for worse, and are leading our children into a way of being we/they can hardly imagine.

Most of our contemporaries tell a different story about designing, in which designers fashion or craft artifacts (including 'information') that others 'use.' One reason that we talk about it this way, I think, is that it can be frightening to contemplate the actual consequences of our actions. Do we dare speak a story in which, in the process of designing structures in which others live, we are designing them, their possibilities, what they attend to, the choices they will make, and so forth?

By steadfastly putting our attention on artifacts, we are also able to escape the harsh light of a difficult adjacent question: Who do we think we are to mess around with others' lives? By what kind of audacity do we set ourselves up in that kind of position in the world? If we puncture the pretense of being involved only in the design of artifacts and the arrangement of activities, and we open ourselves to a fuller recognition of the implications of our designs, then we must ask where to stand to be confident in our judgments about what will be better, or right, for those on whose behalf we design.

Of course we have, ready at hand, two great feints available. On the one hand, we can claim that we are only giving people what they want. That is how we run most of our politics and our marketing, our enterprises, and many other things these days. On the other hand, we have the great argument about the wisdom of the market. We don't need to claim that we have found a right way to do things; we leave it to the market to decide.

I propose we begin to craft another story about designers and what they are doing. Let me point in the direction I am thinking first with an analogy. Several years ago, I warned the community of archivists – the archivist profession – against persisting in the interpretation that the best way to understand what they did was with the distinctions of the computer industry. I told them that if they continued with the story that what they bring to the world is storing and retrieving information, they were going to get what they were asking for: they were going to be replaced by computers, to our universal loss.

We can construct for ourselves a parallel challenge. On what ground shall we stand to design practices – the way that people interpret what they are and do the things they do in the world – if not on the grounds of consensus, fads, market research, or the great wisdom of the market?

For What is the Designer Accountable?

The job of a designer, in my view, is to bring new practices to people. Designs, in the conventional sense of the word, are components, not unities. Ink without a pen is not very interesting, nor is the light bulb without electricity. The relevant unity, when we consider the questions of design, is a practice – human beings in the midst of concernful activities, supported by networks of equipment and help, taking care of things that matter to them.

To put it succinctly, at the end of a successful design project – no matter how modest or grand – we will be able to observe a community of human beings working together in ways that are new to them, and those new ways of working will bring specific incremental (or marginal, to use the economists' term) benefits.

Bringing a New Practice

A number of years ago I invented for myself a way of staying in touch with the way I frame the outcome I aim for in my design work: a practice fully incorporated into a community. It had become clear to me that I was no less susceptible to falling in love with my 'designs' (as components) than anybody else, and that falling in love with a component was a surefire way of wasting my time and that of a lot of other people as well. I called my invention

Five Aspects of Bringing a New Practice.

I named the five: Provocation, Diagnosis, Offer, Mobilization, and Accumulation.

Successful design work, I claim, goes forward in all five of these domains at the same time, in parallel. As has been my practice in inventions such as this one, I selected each word to be slightly awkward and opaque, even to me. This way they are hard to dismiss as simple translations of familiar distinctions. I wanted to avoid having people miss the point of the inventions by saying, "Oh, I see, that's just like this other thing." A diagnosis is not a problem, and an offer is not a solution nor is it a design. You'll see how the five play out in the following short introductions to them. Each time I work with these names I have to re-invent (re-discover) each one. They stay fresh for me. When I introduce them to others, hopefully, they appear less what I remember and recite, and more something invented in our conversation, so we may work together in the space they provide as a living structure.

Let me introduce the five, and then we can see something of their utility.

Provocation

A designer seeking to bring new practices must provide a big provocation, because changing practices is expensive and dangerous. To begin to work in a different way costs money; people lose power and identity; and it takes a substantial human investment to bridge the chasm from old to new. Formerly skillful people lose their reliable stations in life, and upstarts end up with new power. Moreover, it takes more than one provocation. The designer needs at least one sufficient provocation for each party and role that will be involved in and affected by the coming changes. Executives, investors, workers, suppliers, even spouses each have different kinds of concerns, and need provocations to get and keep them involved in positive ways.

To get a community moving on the development of an authentically new set of practices, you need powerful reasons that hang together in a set of stories. Without sufficient provocations, people will invent themselves as indifferent to, or enemies of the changes that the designer is preparing. Finally, the right kinds of provocations are not stable; they change over the course of the project of bringing the new practices. Provocations that are sufficient to create the space of speculation are insufficient for funding a pilot. Provocations sufficient for a pilot are insufficient for constructing a whole new way of working for a whole company, and so forth.

Diagnosis

A successful modification of practices, or an introduction of new practices, always stands on top of a good diagnosis. In the jargon of the age, we provide solutions to problems, and our children are trained in 'problem-solving' in school. If we are purchasing a new brand of pencil, a couch, moving our office, or adding a computer, we do not need a diagnosis. We are making a choice or a decision. Speaking of a 'diagnosis' would be a pretentious way of talking about the analytic process of selecting our new pencil. However, if we are changing essential practices, then we need a powerful diagnostic interpretation about the current situation in which we find ourselves that can allow us to select the right team and design the actions to guide the community as it moves from one world of practices into another. The diagnosis provides an explanation of what gave rise to the current situation in which we find ourselves, and, at the same time, serves as the declaration about the kinds of interventions we will make to change the situation.

Think about a medical team going after some malady arising from unclear or ambiguous origins, for example, an ongoing series of severe head or stomach-aches. The medical team must do the right kinds of tests, articulate a diagnosis in a preliminary way, assemble a team who are competent to act in the space that the diagnosis defines, develop a plan of action, and then manage it and the client to a successful resolution. At its center, a diagnosis is a declaration about the space of interpretation in which a competent team is going to go to work to change something. It does not mean an answer to a problem.

Answers to problems, ultimately, are trivial. A big opportunity needs a good diagnosis, and to move forward without one is effectively to waste the opportunity.

Offers

One needs a series of effective offers, between customers and performers, in which each next offer brings essential conditions for the next step of building the new practice. There are a whole gaggle of customers and performers in this equation. End-customers, investor-customers, employee-customers, ally-customers, executive and manager-customers, and so forth. Taking it incrementally, in order to deal with the fact that people almost never build instantly the kind of trust needed for a major project of changing practices, we see a sequence of steps: a) finish the diagnosis, b) demonstrate the possibility, c) develop a plan of action, d) do a pilot, e) plan the full implementation, and so forth. As each subsequent offer is made and accepted, the resulting exchange of promises (I offer you 'x', in exchange for 'y') produces the force and authority for changes to be made.

Notice that none of our list of five aspects of bringing a new practice is called 'the design.' Characteristically 'the design' is a component in several of the five, most critically the offer. The design provides the grounding for making an offer about where we are headed.

Mobilization

We need a set of activities in which we will build the new practice – bring the new practice into operation in the community. The result of a successful mobilization is not that we finish some artifact or product, but that a community of people is now working in a new way. A mobilization can be easy or hard, and the kinds of foundations with which you start are critical. The central challenges of the mobilization are threaded throughout the other parts of this story: the right provocations, diagnosis, offers, and evidence of the accumulation of capital through the shift in practices. A mobilization is managed through a process of keeping coherence among all aspects of a program for bringing a new practice, fulfilling the promises made in the process, building new habits in the bodies of the people involved, and doing that in a way that does not get caught in the crossfire of old habits that would, otherwise, take the community in a different direction.

Accumulation

The ultimate test of a new practice is that it allows us to accumulate one or more types of capital: financial (money), pragmatic (know-how), or symbolic (identity) capital at a faster rate than before the change of practices. If an investment to produce a new set of practices does not produce an increased flow of one or more kinds of capital, then the change was for the sake of change, and it is just too costly to do that. Changes in the rates of accumulation of capital produced from a new practice will function as important primary provocations for various communities.

The Whole of Design

While I have presented these in a particular order, my recommendation is that the designer keeps all five in his or her attention from the first moment of considering the possibility of a change. The five overlap all over the place in a successful project, and they cannot be accomplished serially. For example, we need to have a plan to accumulate more capital of some sort as part of our provocation, and we all have experience with the way that 'quick hits' – early results – amplify or transform the provocation available to us. Each of the five will be found to be interwoven with the others in analogous ways.

Now, if I say that designers are responsible for bringing new practices, and I recommend that designers design in all five of these domains throughout a project, let us ask where does the work of the designer begin, and where does it end?

My answer is not good news to those who would attempt to do a nice clean division of labor between strategists, designers, builders, commissioners, operators, and maintainers. Each new design brings a set of practices that help a community, institution, or organization accumulate more capital over time. The designer's job spans the lot.

If an implementation fails, it is an error of the designer. If it turns out that there is something in the community that was not visible to the designer that ends up stopping the effectiveness of the design, it is the error of the designer. If a design results in something that, when managed, doesn't produce new capital for the investors, it is a failure of the designer.

For What Do I Want to be Accountable?

Finally, then, I come around to where I stand as a designer. Human beings, it appears to me, are wired for concernful involvement with each other. We arrive in a world already 'designed' for that. Every day, and everywhere we look, we can see things broken, missing, and in the way. Those with the audacity to invent themselves as designers, and with the good fortune to find a place to stand from which to collaborate with others in the design of their lives, will dare to intervene in this world. They will invent new practices, habits, artifacts, tools and systems that will reshape the coordination among us all.

My focus is on improving our capacity to take care of ourselves, each other, and this world. To do this well, we need to stand in history, responsible for ourselves and our interpretations. We need to be competent for inventing new distinctions around which new actions will be brought and coordinated in our new world. We need to be competent for listening to the moods and concerns of those whose lives we will interfere with. We need to be competent for inviting, asking, offering, and all manner of conversations with which we will invite, cajole, guide, and bring those with whom we share an old world as together we traverse to a new world. Change is expensive and dangerous, and those who will join us as we set out for a new world, losing sight of the shore, will be anxious at least, and sometimes downright frightened.

Chapter 5: Leading

For several years, Guillermo Wechsler and I were partners in a consulting firm we called "BABDI". One of our clients was a marvelous young man in Chicago who had invented a business distributing sports-trading cards that had grown nearly overnight to $120 million a year in sales. We wrote this paper to help him navigate the world of management and leadership without the benefit of an MBA and the many years of experience that would have normally put him in condition to manage his business.

While in college, our client had collected cards as a hobby. One day an acquaintance of his, knowing of his interest, asked if he would like, for very little money, a container full of obsolete trading cards that was headed to a pulp mill for recycling. Suspecting that in that mass of cards there might be a significant number of rookie cards of players who had later become successful (which for a collector are valuable), he accepted the offer. His guess was correct. He began repackaging the cards into packets and offered them with the promise of a rookie card in each pack. He bought time on QVC to advertise his cards. He bought other containers of obsolete cards and rapidly found himself the proprietor of a $20-million business. Then he was approached by someone who offered to sell him an agreement with WalMart that allowed him to put kiosks near the cashiers selling his cards in some hundreds of stores. He bought the contract and organized a simple workforce of people to put his products in those stores. Then he went back and re-read the agreement with WalMart and discovered that he had the right to distribute his cards in 2000 stores. Ramping up to do that business, he found himself the proprietor of a $120-million business with 500 employees.

At this point, friends advised him that he needed to hire professional managers for this business, lest he find himself in serious trouble. He hired four very able managers to manage sales, marketing, operations, and finances. Those managers, happy with the business and their new roles. and seeing a bright future ahead of them, decided that the most serious challenge they faced was the inexperience of the founder of the company, and so began to talk to him about moving him out of the senior role he occupied.

On the recommendation of a close friend of our client, Guillermo and I arrived on the scene at that moment. We interviewed the people and reviewed the situation. We concluded that our young client was exactly the right person to lead the company, but that he was missing competence for talking about what he was doing. He was missing competence for leading a sizable and rapidly growing company. Fortunately the new professional managers were ethical people and not greedy to take the company away from its founder. We needed a fast path to preparing our client to lead the company with confidence and skill. What to do? We were not going to tell him to read 1000 books on leadership or do an MBA. So we wrote this short and pithy paper and used it for conversations with him and his management team as we prepared them to work together in new ways. Today this company is well on its way to being a billion dollar company.

Leadership By Design: Fundamental Skills for Creating and Managing Value

By Chauncey Bell and Guillermo Wechsler

> "The opposite of faith is not doubt, but certainty."
>
> – Attributed to Anne Lamott, who attributes it to Teilhard de Jardin, French philosopher and Jesuit priest.
>
> "[Those] … who invented modern management … were trying to produce consistent results on key dimensions expected by customers, stockholders, employees, and other[s], despite the complexity caused by large size, modern technologies, and geographic dispersion. …
>
> Leadership is very different. It does not produce consistency and order…. It produces movement. Throughout the ages, individuals who have been seen as leaders have created change, sometimes for the better, and sometimes not."
>
> – John P. Kotter, (1990). A Force for Change: How Leadership Differs From Management, New York: The Free Press.

In the few pages that follow, we will attempt to enrich the background in which people usually reflect about leadership and design leadership strategies. We are writing this to help clients of ours who find themselves limited by the lack of stable, simple wisdom about how to lead their organizations. A quick search on amazon.com yields 750 books with 'leading' or 'leadership' in their title; 'manage' and 'management' yield another 1150 titles. Where do you start when confronted with hundreds of voices clamoring for your ear? The simple answer is that most of us stop listening. We pick a familiar structure that served us well at some moment in the past, and we repeat it. At the moment that you need to lead, you are not in condition to begin reading for a PhD program.

We intend that these notes make a contribution to executives and designers seeking to nurture and craft their own leadership skills and styles, giving a foundation for designs that are sound and also flexible enough to support distinctive personal differences. Our aim is to create a foundation to nurture productive thought and action about leadership, leading, and leaders. We will introduce a framework of distinctions to allow the reader to make sense of the huge, idiosyncratic body of knowledge already available in the experience of many exceptional practitioners, and in a vast literature.

What Do We Mean by 'Leadership'?

Leadership is a word that evokes controversial interpretations, and often fails to distinguish powerful and reliable actions. There is no consensus (scientific or other) about what the word means. Leadership is not the kind of instrumental distinction that can assure recurrent stable performance as, by contrast, 'electric charge,' 'velocity,' or 'atomic weight.' As a consequence, prescriptions and rules that offer effective leadership are universally incomplete. So, what are we talking about when we talk about leadership? Why are we concerned with leadership? Why should anyone be interested in studying something so obviously not well understood and potentially difficult to grasp?

We suggest leadership belongs to an extended set of skills that allow us to cope with the constitutional instability of our worlds. This instability is a general phenomenon that pervades the whole of human existence. In this paper, however, we will focus our attention only on dealing with instabilities in the worlds of our commercial and social lives. As a beginning, we recommend the reader focus on the concerns that give rise to conversations about leadership, and more attention to questions about leadership than to answers.

Alongside leadership, another big set of skills for coping with constitutional instabilities is called 'management.' Professor John Kotter, Matsushita Professor of Leadership at the Harvard Business School, tells us that "…the pioneers who invented modern management … were trying to produce consistent results on key dimensions expected by customers, stockholders, employees, and other organizational constituencies, despite the complexity caused by large size, modern technologies, and geographic dispersion. … Leadership is very different. It does not produce consistency and order, as the word itself implies. It produces movement. Throughout the ages, individuals who have been seen as leaders have created change, sometimes for the better, and sometimes not."[11]

Leadership – producing movement or change – becomes relevant when our current way of coping with the world is no longer effective. We call for leadership, in the face of substantial changes in an industry, when competitors or new technologies threaten to leave a company behind, when customers are deeply dissatisfied and an organization's responses are not producing results, and when we are attempting to do things for which we do not have good precedents and templates.

The Activities of the Leader

The fundamental activities of the leader are rhetorical and conversational. With these words we point to the activities of cultivating, adjusting, and enriching the discursive distinctions, semantic

---

[11] John P. Kotter, (1990). A Force for Change: How Leadership Differs From Management, New York: The Free Press, A Division of Macmillan, Inc., p. 4. In October 2001, Business Week magazine rated Kotter the #1 "Leadership Guru" in America, based on a survey they conducted of 504 enterprises.

wording, and expressions that produce rich sensitivities for grasping concerns of others, and allows the leader to produce strong impacts in audiences. Leaders change people's orientations in conversations: conversations with individuals and groups, face to face and through writing or other media, but always focusing on listening.

Effective leaders listen to how others listen, and challenge and shape their own listening and that of their audiences. Leadership, in short, is about changing social conversations and articulating emerging concerns. Listening is the most important aspect of leadership. It is also usually the most difficult, because people take listening for granted. The world gives little attention to teaching what listening is or how to do it, and we assume that leaders, leading, must do most of the talking. In keeping silent, letting others talk, asking questions, and creating an open and trusting background, leaders create room for unusual conversations to show up.

Leaders also trigger changes in the background in which conversations happen by declaring[12] what needs attention, crises, and emergencies, and creating new experiences. Then they listen to how others listened to what they said. Leaders attune their commitments and rhetoric to affect others' listening and to create opportunities for others to engage with the strategic agenda they are leading. Leaders alter the way that others listen by helping them embrace new concerns (and co-inventing new concerns with them) that will orient them to the future in a more meaningful and powerful way. This dimension of leadership activity is born in three rich human traditions: economics, ethics and the constitution of personal and social identities.

---

[12] 'Declaration' – to declare – is the name we give to one of six classes of 'performative' language actions with which we human beings invent our worlds and coordinate with each other to produce action in them. The English philosopher John L. Austin (1911-1960) was the first to notice the existence of a class of verbs that he called performatives[– verbs that, rather than describing actions, perform actions. When someone says "I promise to …," he is performing the action of promising, not reporting that he will, did, or might promise. It turns out that all human languages contain performatives. For the purpose of designing work in organizations, we distinguish six classes of performatives: declarations, offers, requests, promises, assessments, and assertions. Ask the authors for more on the subject.

For the competent leader, leadership is actually quite simple. It is a conversational skill. However, it is not easily learned, and the exercise of leadership is overwhelmingly complex if you don't know what to watch. The central challenge on the way to competence is to learn to observe how people invent alternative futures in their conversations with other people with seriousness and discipline. This conversational dimension of leadership is not accessible without first training yourself in certain ways of observing what happens as people speak and listen to each other – how futures are invented in conversations.

With this background, we now point to seven sets of practices that leaders cultivate. We use the word 'practices' to alert the reader that we are not simply talking about 'things to do,' 'tools,' or 'tips and techniques.' Think of "the practice of medicine" or the "practice of engineering." The word practice points in a holistic way to a collection of intricately harmonized actions, the background in which those actions happen, tools, institutions and curricula of education and governance, habits of thinking and acting in a community, and ethical orientations among the principal dimensions in which action is happening.

To enter a practice one enters a community that embodies or takes care of that practice, finds someone there who is willing to help develop the practice, and follows his or her instructions. In other words, find the right mentor and open a space in which to be mentored. Great leaders do not spring fully articulated from nowhere; they are mentored by others who help them build their own practices of leadership.

First: Reading the World

Leaders have practices for 'reading' the world – listening to what is going on around them – and for sorting through (and examining) the multiplicity of narratives that configure their worlds and shape their possibilities. Narratives – the recurring threads of the stories that people tell about their worlds and their roles in those worlds, including what we see and what we don't see as actors in those stories – are not merely descriptive. On the contrary, our narratives are the stuff of our opportunities. We do not judge narratives by their accuracy or comprehensiveness, but by their capacity to re-connect and re-couple worlds in a way that we see new ways of understanding our pasts, new bridges to the future, and new endings. It is in our narratives that new, uncertain, yet exciting possible futures have the opportunity to capture the hearts of communities, teams, and business networks. In interpreting and shaping stories, the leader creates new worlds, opportunities, paths to the future, and the meanings and obstacles to be removed. In this sense, storytelling is re-plotting the business space so new exchanges and new practices can be invented. Obviously in speaking of storytelling in this way, we do not mean idle journalistic reportage, gossip, or surveys of opinions. We are pointing to carefully crafted distinctions and interpretations that unleash previously unnoticed resources and impact the current world, distinguishing new spaces of possibilities and new spaces for action.

Second: Managing Power

Leaders accumulate, exercise, and manage power. We use the word 'power' in a very specific way – as an assessment of the capacity of an individual or organization to take action. Someone with more power is able to produce a result with more efficiency, speed, or quality than someone else. We judge leaders by the richness of the possibilities inherent in the worlds they are capable of bringing to life; power is essential for bringing possibilities to fruition. Organizations and institutions accumulate many kinds of power. We particularly distinguish three, and measure the accumulation of power as 'capital:'

1. *Financial Capital* (based in institutional promises) gives the holder the capacity to make requests in marketplaces.

2. *Know-how, or pragmatic capital* (individual and social capacities organized as networks of roles, skills, equipment, and technologies to deliver specific results and performance) gives the capacity to make and fulfill unique offers that are valuable to others.

3. *Symbolic capital* (identities, recognition, and reputation that give access to networks and resources) gives the capacity of being listened and recognized in a singular way.

We understand power in a different way than the traditional naïve moralistic assessment Westerners often attach to the notion. For example, a friend of ours makes a big distinction between leadership understood in 'domination' and 'partnership paradigms.' For us, this is a moralistic interpretation, attempting to escape distaste for the exercise of power. Neither side of the distinction works. People need leaders. Obviously we don't want them to dominate us. Neither do we want them to be our partners – not really – we want them to lead, out ahead of us. We do not expect our leaders to be our equals, performing the same actions that we perform; nor do we expect our leaders to live by exactly the same rules that apply to our behavior as members of the community. In many Western countries in which egalitarianism has become a dominant virtue, we prefer to be led by someone more "like us," but even then we apply somewhat different rules (sometimes stricter) to the behavior of our leaders.

Politics is the senior power conversation. Politics is a conversational activity that focuses on engaging different sources of power to mobilize interests and actions with some strategic purpose. Effective political conversation requires leaders to reinterpret available resources from new perspectives, to enable new possibilities to emerge and new power to be accumulated. Governmental politics is about accumulating capital for the sake of building collective identities. Of course, this interpretation stands in stark contrast to how we commonly think about politics in the United States. In modern democracies, we recognize individuals as legitimate agents with specific rights and duties. Politics in business and commerce is about building collective identities, participating as particular role identities, inventing and completing exchange conversations to produce value for the parties involved.

Failing to exercise power while leading usually leads to unhappy consequences.

Third: Producing Unsettlement

Effective leaders have rich practices for producing and managing unsettlement. The central point of this set of practices is the capacity it gives the leader to attack and dissolve parts of the current common sense, demolish current certainties – things that people previously had confidence in – and create space for new questions to emerge, new ways of listening, and new issues to be taken in account. Leaders produce unsettlement in different ways: sophisticated humor, brutal breakdowns, pitiless assessments and declarations, or carefully crafted analysis. How the unsettlement is produced is far less important than having the capacity to produce it and keep people unsettled as long as necessary to produce a new background. The unsettlement we speak of gives space for capitalizing emerging opportunities. We can see in this set of capacities – producing unsettlement and holding it in place – the reason that leaders are often caricatured as rule-breakers, challengers of established values, or possessed of difficult behaviors. In the right moment, after the unsettlement has done its job, effective leaders also declare new certainties that subsequently orient questioning, lead people to a new appreciation of the business situation, and re-orient operational actions.

Leaders don't just produce unsettlement about the future that is coming. They are just as likely to undermine interpretations about the past, producing unsettlement about how we have interpreted ourselves as a way of orienting people to the worlds they are trying to build. Strong leaders have a remarkable capacity to tune themselves with strong historical discourses and rebuild their practices and rhetoric out of them. We can think of a few leaders that have led their communities through not just one or two, but many competitive and technical challenges, and sometimes even multiple changes in the communities' cultural and historical backgrounds.

A critical aspect of this is the capacity for self-transformation found in many of our greatest leaders. Effective leaders often act out of the conviction that the reinvention of their business is also, simultaneously and inevitably, the reinvention of themselves, including the unsettlement, uncertainty and struggle that always accompanies such transformations. These leaders engage in conversations in which they transform themselves to become critical nodes in emerging value-generating networks. A friend of ours who works as an elected official rebuilds herself and her network every year or so. She used to complain of the effort; now she just does it. Such people pay attention to the past, but not merely as mandate and set of values to be treasured and projected. They look to the past as the source of possibilities to be shaped into new roles in which to play in the networked world they move. It is true that leaders often leave themselves open to the characterization that they are ethically flexible and creative, but this does not mean that an effective leader can be rootless, merely opportunistic, or nihilistic. An effective leader's relationship with what is unknown is extremely friendly; not knowing is an asset in the hands of a skilled leader. Expanding our ignorance is the only chance we have for something new to emerge.

Fourth: Building Conversations in which Markets are Expanded or Invented

Leaders develop the networks of conversation in which possibilities are invented. To do this, they bring forth (elicit, evoke, and speak) basic commitments among people in a very peculiar fashion.

1. They articulate new and unusual products and services, and ways of measuring the contributions that people make in developing and delivering them – sometimes turning the world on its head. For an example in government politics, remember John F. Kennedy: "And so, my fellow Americans: ask not what your country can do for you - ask what you can do for your country." (Inaugural Address, Jan. 20th 1961)

2. They declare (bring into existence) roles that do not belong to the current world. For example, the modern versions of human resources, information technology, logistics, shared services, and outsourcers are roles invented in the last 50 years by leaders committed to bringing new concerns and new organizations of work. *[Chauncey's note in July of 2020: The pandemic is calling on today's leaders to do this kind of work now, and faster than we have been used to in making these kinds of changes for the last many decades.]*

3. They invent new "bridging narratives" – new stories that help people make the leap from the present to a future with different concerns, different values and wastes, and consequently changed structures of influence and power for those who live in the new world.

Leaders engage in conversations embodying a peculiar understanding of language. In general terms, they don't treat language as a passive device to describe the world. They are not constrained by passive-descriptive interpretations. On the contrary, our best leaders understand language as a generative practice.[13] Explicitly or implicitly, leaders invent themselves in the conviction that worlds are invented in networks of conversations that they influence or lead – networks in which opportunities are invented and action is mobilized. In this sense, leaders' practices for thinking and acting are social; they do not think about themselves as isolated, autonomous agents. Their conversational practices allow them to get in contact with relevant networks, to develop new networks, and to couple networks in unusual ways. Faced with a big challenge, a leader's attention will quickly turn to questions about the networks they need to develop, what conversations will produce the right opportunities, and how to assemble or access and nurture those networks. Leaders are sensitive to the quality of their conversations, the trust that makes certain conversations possible (or not), the way that trust is built or damaged in those conversations, and the emotional backgrounds that hold and orient the conversational foreground.

It makes no difference whether those conversational networks are simple, as when dealing with office space issues, or complex, as outsourcing a billion-dollar business. Some conversational networks require sophisticated technological platforms; others are (apparently simple) face-to-face interactions. Some conversational networks require years of preparation; others happen in seconds.

Fifth: Bringing Resolution and Action

Leaders have efficient practices to bring resolution and produce action through conversations. They declare and manage speculative conversations to create possibilities. They organize and manage transitions from people's experience of frustration or excitement to sets

---

[13] Many people have influenced our thinking on this subject. The most important influences have been Fernando Flores, Hubert Dreyfus, Friedrich Nietzsche, John Austin, Paul Ricoeur, Martin Heidegger, and Hannah Arendt.

of articulated concerns; from spaces of possibilities to specific articulated opportunities. They declare the routes and schedules for engaging in decisive conversations for action. They declare experimental projects to allow those concerned to better understand emerging opportunities, and they declare strategic projects to produce significant reconfigurations of businesses. They declare their concerns and point to relevant features of the future they are attempting to construct. They define the space in which they are interested in receiving offers. They dissolve hidden negative moods of ungrounded hope, resignation, skepticism, overwhelm and the like. They invest in mobilizing action and removing the friction that produces something less than total commitment to impeccable execution. Speaking broadly, leaders carefully manage conversations that maintain, expand, or repair trust in the relationships that allow their companies to adjust themselves to different futures – the conversations that allow their organizations to maintain respect, loyalty, and conviction.

Sixth: Mentoring People

Leaders carefully balance the institutional capabilities of their organizations and the capabilities of key individual performers. They are skilled at mentoring the people who will be key players in the games they are inventing. Individual contributors can be relevant for their technical skills, their business knowledge and relationships, or for their work ethic or style of working. Leaders usually include pivotal individual contributors in a special network of conversations in which exchanges (compensation and sharing of revenues) are designed in ways that incent both execution and loyalty. In moments of important challenges and transition, key individual performers embody the organization's struggles in different ways. Some embody the future, as key participants in the process of bringing a different world; others embody the past and act as guardians protecting historical virtues and sources of value; and some serve on bridges, bringing new practices that will allow the organization to go from the past to the future successfully.

Leaders push people to grow by producing big and challenging breakdowns and providing some of the right resources for people to thrive.

Seventh: Navigating in Technology

The modern leader has practices to interact with technologists, invest effectively in the development of technology, and design ways for new technologies to help bring new futures. The particular technologies that are going to be relevant depend upon the industry in which one works. For example, we have worked with clients whose businesses depended upon their intimate involvement with metallurgy, high altitude maintenance and logistics (mining), genetics and botany (agricultural businesses), chemistry (cement and pharmaceuticals). On the other hand, 'information technology' – IT – is an essential technology in every industry today. It is no longer possible to lead significant communities in the world without the intervention, intermediation, and support of IT. Fifty years ago, 'IT' meant machines oriented to storing and retrieving information. Twenty five years ago the focus of the technology morphed to communication. Today, when you look closely you see that the technology is centrally concerned with the delivery of services. Leaders use this technology to bring new worlds, shape the opportunities and worlds they bring, and intervene in rigidities in the worlds they seek to change. Information technology today expands the capacity of organizations to participate in business conversations around the world – conversations in which business opportunities are declared, deals are articulated, consummated, and networks of commitments are activated to complete deals and deliver services and products.

Frequently people find interacting with technology and technologists intimidating. You are attempting to navigate – find your way – in fields that are changing with great speed, where resources and advisors are extremely expensive, and the risks of mis-steps look potentially lethal. Very occasionally, effective leaders are also senior practitioners in technological fields that are deeply related to the work of their enterprises. Usually, however, this is not the case, even in many cases when it appears to be.

The most effective leaders develop practices and skills for doing something very curious: making effective assessments in matters and domains where they are not competent. This sounds contradictory, but here is a real-life example that shows the dimensions of it. Anyone who has had a serious chronic medical condition or medical emergency has encountered the situation where you find that you must take action, authorize others to take action, or set in place life-changing decisions on the basis of recommendations from other people that we have not known for a long time. What you discover in those moments, if you are lucky and paying attention, is that you must navigate by 1) putting yourself in touch with the right networks of practitioners (i.e., in the hands of the right doctors), 2) making careful assessments about the capacity of the people you are working with to make effective assessments about the situation in which you find yourself, and 3) having the right people construct for you maps of the whole domain in which you are navigating, so that you can spot things that are changing and know better how to protect and take care of yourself.

Afterword

We do not pretend to encompass the whole phenomenon of leadership with the seven practices introduced in this short paper. Rather, we wanted to open some avenues for exploration. As you explore these seven basic sets of practices you are not at the end of the task. On the contrary, you are just opening a new way of dealing with what we indicate with the word 'leadership.' Even though you are just starting, if you explore seriously, we are confident that this framework will fit well with your intuitions and will open a whole new horizon for designing how to generate value.

One more dimension of leadership is this: leaders embody the tension – or better, the collision – between assuring current business viability and coupling with emerging market spaces to craft new business identities. Another way of saying this is that leaders deal with all parts of the collision between nurturing current roles and configuring spaces in which new roles can emerge.

Leadership is a significant task that calls for challenging the current common sense and unsettling basic certainties. The leader works in many dimensions: removing operational waste, prototyping new offers, developing new capacities, mobilizing operational innovations, assuring business results, affecting the cultural background, and developing key people among others. Oddly, at the same time a sound Leadership Strategy is not constructed from a program of components, but rather emerges as something simple that touches the heart of the business enterprise with a few decisive initiatives that change the game and the background in which it is played.

To develop your capacity for leadership, one of your key challenges will be the rigor with which you build each relevant practice, and, on the other hand, the rigor with which you use the outcomes of your actions as a source of new questions, for tuning your designs. In many traditions for understanding leaders and leadership, the leader is a solitary individual who, by accident, discipline, or other reason developed his or her skill as a leader. We are not recommending work on yourself in this tradition. Discipline and good fortune are advantages for a leader, and Louis Pasteur's wise "Chance favors the prepared mind" is a good ironic warning. However, we do not advise that you attempt to develop yourself as a leader by yourself. Leadership is a phenomena that arrives and thrives in social and historical networks, and not merely in individual bodies.

Chapter 6: Listening

My essay on 'Navigating' begins with this sentence:

> *My mother, my father, Rose, Sibble, and Carnell Eaton pre-pared me to listen to people including those very different than myself.*

In the beginning of our lives we learn to listen as we interact with our parents (or with those serving in those roles). I consider this sensibility – listening to people different from myself – to have been one of the most important early gifts of my life.

My father was an engineer's engineer, a magnificent human being who moved through his adult life from being a hyper-technocrat to being a great lover of human beings. He met my mother Kay when she was 16 at a coming-out event in New York City. Enchanted, he proposed to her. She told him he was crazy; she wasn't old enough to do that! But she invited him to stay in communication until she grew up. He did.

My mother thought she would become an artist; she became the wife of an engineer and designer, a mother, and a courageous speaker in every world she encountered. She was my first best friend and taught me critical parts of having friends including building trust, paying attention to others, loyalty, and betrayal.

Rose, whose last name is now lost to me, and Sibble Hawthorne were Kay's 'maids' during my early years, Rose in Baltimore and Sibble in Los Angeles. Rose traveled every day from Baltimore's black ghetto to Roland Park to work as Kay's partner in our household. Sibble, who had previously been a police officer in Los Angeles and Yul Brenner's chauffeur, was Kay's partner in our home from the time I was 10 until I went to college.

Carnell Eaton, a sophisticated man of color from Roxbury, Massachusetts came to the offices of Arthur D. Little, Inc. while I was working there. He asked the company to send someone to a workshop he was inventing to address the racial struggles going on in Boston. The situation in Boston at the time was similar to what is going on in many major cities in the fall of 2020 as I write this. My bosses agreed to support what he was doing and I accepted their invitation to attend. In the opening of the workshop, Carnell asked each of us about our histories. When his digging revealed that I had been brought up in the Roland Park neighborhood of Baltimore, Maryland and Tarzana, California, and had attended Harvard School and Harvard College, he quipped "I did not think that people like you actually existed; I thought they made up them up in books!" He recognized the character of those neighborhoods and schools as very different from his world.

Before I met him, Carnell had spent 14 years in Massachusetts prisons for bank robbery. While in prison he had become a student of David McClelland, a famous organizational consultant, who chaired the Department of Social Relations at Harvard. In the weeks and months that followed our meeting, this magnificent man and I became business partners. Our partnership was cut short when he was murdered by members of his community who were jealous of his influence and power.

Rose, Sibble, and Carnell all had brown skin and belonged to communities that were segregated from mine by space and culture. By

their examples, kindnesses, listening, and fierce pride as human beings they were strong and wise early teachers for me.

At the beginning of the new millennium my wife Shirah and I committed to write an essay together on listening as an exercise for exploring our concerns, our marriage, our concern for our children, and
to do something valuable together. In addition to her PhD in business from Stanford, and our both being students of Fernando Flores, Shirah had spent several years studying in the tradition called
Spiritual Direction[14], sometimes called 'holy listening,' and was cer-
tified as a Spiritual Director. In my work with Fernando, I had
watched him at one moment call into question everything that we
thought we understood about listening. Working with Hubert Dreyfus and Charles Spinosa he undertook a kind of archeological investigation of listening. Meanwhile, I had discovered Gemma Corradi Fiumara's wonderful (and challenging) book The Other Side of
Language: A Philosophy of Listening[15] and had spoken briefly to
the author on the phone.

Shirah and I went to work researching and drafting. We discovered
that the vast majority of what is written on the subject of listening is
actually about the concern for talking effectively, and not about the
phenomena of listening. We discovered the International Listening
Association (ILA). We joined it and applied to speak at their annual
meeting in Stockholm. Our proposal was accepted. We travelled
there and led a session at their annual meeting. We discovered in
that adventure more about just how slippery the phenomena of listening are. The organization could just as well have been named the
International Oratorical Association. For the most part, the question

---

[14] Spiritual direction is an established but little-known practice of being with people as they strive
to deepen their relationship with the divine, and to learn and grow in their own personal spirituality.
Originally developed in the Catholic tradition, it has expanded to Protestant and Jewish traditions as
well.

[15] Routledge, 1995.

on peoples' minds was how to affect listening, how to speak more effectively, and not what is actually going on when human beings are listening.

For our presentation in Stockholm we prepared a talk and exercises for the ILA. We did not actually present this paper. Our time on the dias would not have allowed it, and the audience would not have been prepared to digest it. Over time this paper has become for me what in today's jargon might be understood as a portal or a platform for several things. It has been foundational in the marriage Shirah and I have now conducted for more than 37 years, a background in which I stand as I listen to people in my work, my communities, and my family, and a flag identifying a territory in which continuous exploration has been valuable to me.

Before reading further, I recommend you review my provocation on listening found in Chapter 2. There I have introduced listening in a way that may make it easier to fully enjoy and benefit from this essay.

Listening and Anxiety in Designing a Life

Chauncey Bell and Shirah Bell, PhD November, 2002

In this paper we explore anxiety: how it shows up as an ally when we are undertaking changes, what its virtues and dangers are and how to interact with it. After that, we will connect anxiety with listening: introduce what we think listening is, explore the role listening plays as we undertake changing ourselves and our circumstances, and finally make some recommendations for future action.

We Can Count on Change

Change is one of the few things we count on today. We live in the midst of an ongoing avalanche of actions and opportunities. How, we wonder, shall we cope? How can we 'manage' the change, mitigate it, contain it, surf the avalanche? How can we proactively introduce changes to move our lives in the direction we want them to go? How can we intercede in the natural drift of life? We come upon the concern with 'design' when we undertake a commitment to change our practices or the drift of our lives.

Change produces unsettledness or anxiety in our bodies. To some degree, this unsettledness is always there; at every moment we have the rest of our lives in front of us, and we cannot be certain about the future. We particularly notice the unsettledness when something important to us is changing or we sense something is about to change. It is commonplace today to talk about all the changes, our unsettledness, and how anxious we are. Perhaps the anxiety and unsettledness are hallmarks of our modern society.

In the process of confronting aspects of our lives and circumstances with which we are not satisfied – as we prepare to 'design' – we encounter, precipitate. or provoke anxiety in ourselves and sometimes in others. As Chauncey sometimes says to his clients and students, "If no one is anxious, you can be pretty sure nothing important is changing." If you're looking at the people you're working with, and everyone is comfortable, then it is likely you are not doing anything that will change the circumstances around you. If something that matters is happening, then people will be unsettled. They will experience physical sensations to which they will give different names, such as excitement, alarm, fear, or anticipation. To improve our capacity to design, understanding what is going on with the unsettledness that we call anxiety is pretty important.

Why Listening?

As we undertake to make changes, it is just as important to understand what is going on in what we are going to call listening. As we prepare to make things happen and construct new practices, before anything of any consequence happens, we are already listening and speaking. Our common sense is that what makes things happen is ideas, meetings, plans, designs, proposals, tools, procedures, and the like – all actions of speaking. Today we talk a lot about the impact of new technological tools on our lives, especially computers, cell phones, PDAs, and the Internet. Closer examination reveals that the changes in our lives come from new opportunities these tools give us to communicate differently with each other, and not from the tools themselves. Talking about the changes that the tools are bringing is a shorthand. With these tools, we are speaking and listening in ways that were previously unavailable, with the consequence that we are changing what we do, how we do it, and from there how we understand ourselves and each other. It is true that the new ways of understanding ourselves require the new tools, but it is a serious mistake to attribute the instigation of the change to inanimate things.

Even when we pay attention to our actions in language, we focus on speaking, not listening. We tend to think of reporting, analyzing, decision-making, and planning as foundational. We put our attention on more skillful speaking. In meetings, those who are quiet (maybe listening) are often assessed negatively. We attribute success to genius, authority, political savvy, etc. Most of our metaphors in business are of battles, debates, and argumentation[16]. These are all part of what we call 'the speaking side of language,' which predominates in our culture.

---

[16] See especially Deborah Tannen, The Argument Culture, 1998, Random House, Inc. Tannen is the author of You Just Don't Understand, June 1990, William Morrow & Co. in which she explored the difficulty of communications among men and women.

We propose that the other side of language, listening, is the critical variable in success in life and business far more often than anyone suspects. Not only is listening more often the primary, yet hidden, source of our difficulties, but we can also do something to improve listening much more easily than creating more intelligence, genius, or finding solutions by running computer simulations. When listening is happening, thinking, communicating, and collaborating are far simpler. If listening is not happening, most of life is extraordinarily difficult.

When we say "listening is happening" most readers will assume they know what we are talking about. Everyone already has some interpretation of listening. However, the current commonsensical understandings of listening are at best misleading. In the following, we will open the question of what is happening when we are listening (including the moods or predispositions in which we listen, and the interpretations that we make) and contrast that to the current common sense.

Different Kinds of Anxiety

The popular modern notion of anxiety began with Freud[17]. He distinguished three types of anxiety that he called reality, neurotic, and moral. Reality anxiety revolves around the fear of tangible dangers one expects to encounter, such as a tiger about to leap upon us. This type was not particularly interesting to Freud. He focused on neurotic and moral anxiety, which he said had to do with emotional conflicts that were not based in 'reality' and resulted in abnormal behavior and suffering. Freud explained these types of anxiety with what he understood as scientific models depicting 'causes' and 'reasons' for

---

[17] We are introducing Freud here only to show how his approach has pervaded modern Western culture and thinking. We do not intend to do an exposition or analysis of his work.

feelings. He postulated a whole system of psychological constructs (for example, id, ego, super-ego), with which he explained how people become anxious. His basic stance was that these kinds of anxiety were pathological and should be eliminated. Freud's influence has been pervasive. Our common sense is that anxiety is undesirable.

Today, anxiety disorders, ranging from mild worry to recurrent panic attacks, are on center stage. Time Magazine put Understanding Anxiety on its June 10, 2002 cover. Time claimed that anxiety disorders are the most common forms of mental illness in the U.S. Interesting research is being done in brain physiology to ascertain why some people are debilitated by their anxiety while others are not. Psychotherapists who treat anxiety usually attempt to eliminate it. Some therapists acknowledge that a little 'appropriate' anxiety is healthy, but the main thrust of the therapeutic caseload on anxiety is towards finding causes and getting rid of both symptoms and causes. In this paper, we are not going to address pathological, recurrent, debilitating anxieties. However, to avoid confusion, we needed to distinguish them before we can begin to talk about a different kind of anxiety. We will explore a manifestation and interpretation of anxiety that is normal and valuable. To begin our exploration, we will move away from the psychological realm to philosophy.

Anxiety as a Normal Part of Life

In this next part of our paper we will introduce the reader to a constructive role that anxiety plays in each of our lives. This constructive role is so central that we would be crippled without it. We will explore where this anxiety is born, how it shows up in our lives, and how it functions. From there, we will introduce what we will call 'virtuous' anxiety – where anxiety appears as essential instrumentation in 'the designer's toolkit.'

Kierkegaard and Heidegger, contemporary philosophers, were particularly interested in a kind of 'anxiety' that they understood as a normal response to the potentially terrifying uncertainty of the human condition. The more deeply we inquire into life, the more uncertain and ungrounded it reveals itself to be. At the end, there are no immutable rules of behavior that must be followed, no fundamental goals that must be achieved, and no systems of explanation that sit upon universal laws of the universe. Our interpretations of ourselves and each other do not stand on 'facts', but rather on other structures of interpretations. We begin our interpretation of ourselves and each other with the interpretations of our parents and our cultures, and we add our own experience on top of and in opposition to that. The physical world also stands on structures of historical interpretations.

Let's look at a couple of examples. Take the question of what holds the earth in its position in space. Galileo's questions about an earth-centered universe were interpreted as heresy and he was tried for it.

The 'truth' at that moment in history was that God placed and cared for the heavenly bodies. We moderns are more sophisticated. We believe that our physical world was created and flung into space with the big bang, that we have been traveling and evolving since, and that earth is held in position in our solar system by the gravitational attraction between earth and the sun. Is this the 'truth?' Far from it. This is just one more current interpretation. Newton invented gravity. Before he did so, gravity did not exist in the world. Certainly there was a physical force, but by inventing the distinction 'gravity' Newton transformed the possibility of that force. He invented a new way of understanding the universe and in so doing new possibilities for existence showed up.

You may be saying to yourself something to the effect of "OK, we don't understand gravity yet, but science is getting there, we just don't have all the facts." The opposite is the case. The physics that we are taught in high school and college is a domain of facts. The physics of those who are inventing modern physics is a domain of questions and interpretations. Einstein said, "Physical concepts are free creations of the human mind, and are not, however it may seem, uniquely determined by the external world."[18] Living in full recognition of

---

[18] Einstein, A., and Infeld, L., The Evolution of Physics, New York, Simon & Schuster,1938, p.33.

this ungroundedness can be (to say the least) a bit anxiety-provoking.

We don't need to go all the way to confronting the ungroundedness of physics to encounter the source of this kind of anxiety. We can see it in a second example that will be more familiar to all of us, asking ourselves why we are doing what we are doing.

At some moment, a friend – let's say she is a doctor – wonders, "Why am I a doctor?" After some thought, she concludes it is because she likes helping people heal. But then she asks, "Why do I like helping people?" An answer comes: "Well, my mother was very kind and was a role model for me. Another question follows: "Why was she kind?" "She was religious and believed that was the right way to behave." "Why was that the right way to behave?" This questioning can go on and on. Ultimately, we recognize that who we say we are and why we do what we do, are constructed from, and rest upon, a structure of stories that we tell and have been told. They do not stand on solid ground. We can get satisfied with these kinds of answers, but only for a while, and our satisfaction will go away when we ask the next question about why we say each new explanation.

In the end, the only satisfying answer to such questions becomes: "Because I said so. I chose this interpretation, and I (do or will commit to) live my life in a way that is consistent with this interpretation." In the end, our answers to these questions are interpretations, whether we appropriated them from others ("my mother always said I had a nurturing heart"), or invented them for ourselves.

Many of us, at various moments in our lives, are able to recognize and take responsibility for life as an invention we make and then live into. Anxiety of the type in which we are interested here appears in the moment that we acknowledge that our lives are inventions and we cannot know the truth about them. As we live our lives, they are revealed as ungrounded, and that is unsettling. Often this shows up when we interpret that the survival of what we most care about is at stake – when our interpretation of ourselves, our identity, our body, our community, our expectations about the future are unstable, even under attack.

Anxiety in the Clothing of Everyday Fears and Worries

We distinguish this 'normal' anxiety from most of what Freud spoke of, including 'reality anxiety.' For a moment, to simplify, consider any emotion that shows up in response to some specific danger, real or imagined, as the emotion called 'fear'[19]. When we get rid of the danger, the fear begins to pass. Anxiety, as we are speaking of it, is more fundamental, found in the background where we expect to find moods, ready to be triggered in the face of our uncertainty concerning what we care about. From this point forward in this paper we will use the word 'anxiety' to refer only to this particular kind of 'normal' anxiety.

Now this normal anxiety often lurks behind everyday fears and worries, and that can be confusing. We can detect the presence of the anxiety by the ways it distorts and exaggerates what would otherwise be emotional reactions with which we are prepared to deal. For example, Shirah sometimes starts to get fearful about not having enough money to retire. When the fear shows up and she begins to look for the reason for having the fear at the particular moment, not infrequently she finds no obvious change that triggered it – no drop in the stock market, no change in our earning capacity, etc. She has learned to interpret fear appearing in this kind of situation as revealing an anxiety about life. She is anxious about getting older, uncertainty about where we will live, and the state of her health,

---

[19] We'll say something about how we distinguish moods and emotions later in the paper.

etc. The fear of not having enough money is a 'cover' for the anxiety born in those deeper concerns. When Shirah began to recognize this pattern, she stopped scurrying around trying to change our investment strategy, or cut our budget, and began to interact with the anxiety itself. (Sometimes the anxiety lurks behind fears that appear grounded, too. The stock market drops, and the fear starts. However, when she examines the fear, she discovers that although grounded, it is exaggerated, and has been shaped by our friend, 'normal' anxiety.)

Even though normal anxiety often sits beside or evokes fear, when we begin to see it for what it is – it opens up new opportunities for us. It gives us more freedom. We will say more about this in a little bit below. The converse is also the case: to ignore the phenomenon reduces our freedom. This has more immediate consequences. If we design changes for ourselves and those in our lives and we do not take into account the kinds of anxiety that are always present in our bodies and those around us in the right ways, we will find our projects failing or underperforming. Anxiety is a powerful force in the relations among people working and living together. Unattended to, it most frequently pulls us back into old structures of interaction. Attended to, it guides us to paths of opportunity for change.

Many of us can remember encountering a situation in which we or someone else began using a new set of tools in ways that imitated the way we used the tools they replaced, and later discovered that we were losing most of the benefits of the new tools. It was difficult, for example, to use early word processors as typewriters. It was hard to adjust the paper, for example, and the backspace key didn't work as well as the 'correct' button on an IBM Selectric typewriter.

Let's look at an organizational example. Recently Chauncey led a team that designed, built, and installed a new set of tools for a bank to manage and track the progress of every customer request to its successful resolution. The point was to build a set of banking practices that would allow the bank to recognize its customers and manage the context of its relationship with those customers. We were interested in ending the situation where when you call the bank to ask them to fix something, you meet a bureaucracy through which you are expected to navigate. When you ask this new bank for something, the bank will have the capacity to remember what you asked, and to track for you what is happening with your request, rather than forcing you to manage your request until it is complete.

Just as you can go to the UPS or Federal Express website and see where your package has gotten in its delivery cycle because its routing and movement through the network has been managed and recorded by a computer system, the bank's people would be able to observe the progress of work on behalf of customers as that work was routed and tracked from office to office on a computer system. The tools also flagged overdue and pending work. Depending upon its importance for the bank and the particular customer, the tools dynamically re-routed the work to people who could get it done, and gave warning to those who needed to know that the work could or would be late. We designed these tools to make it possible to run a bank that made and fulfilled promises to its customers, to enable the bank to move into the next era of financial services with a capacity to build trust with customers.

The design team knew that the bank's people were anxious about doing new things; anxious about how their supervisors and financial managers would evaluate their work in their departments. Unsettled with all the newness of opening a new bank (in a tremendous hurry), the managers 'fled' into the everyday activity with which they were familiar, using the new tools to do old things in old ways. We seriously underestimated the effect and force of their anxiety. Shortly after the bank's managers started using the tools, we discovered they were using them as if they were fax machines. A request from a customer to the call center was entered into the system and printed out on paper in the back office. No routing, no tracking, no alerts, no warnings, no way of observing progress. The bank continued to manage its work by going through stacks of paper in each department every day.

Another, more successful example of interacting with the anxiety of managers and employees happened several years ago when Chauncey promised the CFO of a large integrated chemical company that he and his colleagues would train a group of his managers and executives to radically reduce the working capital required to run his business. "As we were working with the managers of a division of the company early in the engagement, I discovered that every one of the managers believed that the critical reason for their problems had to do with the CEO's single-minded, autocratic focus on quarterly results for which he was famous. They told me he would not allow them to make any changes that might endanger quarterly results, even if they were convinced that taking such a risk was the only path to a different future. I could see that as a result of this interpretation, they had two paths open to them: do some project surreptitiously, probably failing, or attempt to do a project that I knew would take six months in much less time so that it would show positive results within the quarter. I was sure the second path would fail. I confronted them with what I saw as a shallow interpretation of the concerns and wisdom of the CEO, and said that I would arrange for him to tell them directly his concerns in the matter. I met with the CFO and CEO, asked the CEO to visit this management team and tell them that he wanted them to develop, successfully, a new way of managing their business that conserved working capital, and that he understood that in order to do that they might have to take some risks, violate some traditional rules, and that they might have to go through a period of poorer results to get to the goal. He opened his calendar, scheduled the meeting, opened his notebook, asked me to tell him exactly what I wanted him to tell the team, and wrote himself notes about the talk he was to give. Six months later, the team had built a whole new set of practices for the company."

Here is one more example that we will talk more about later in the paper. Cemex is one of the world's great cement companies. The situation when Chauncey and his colleagues arrived to help them with concrete delivery in Guadalajara and Mexico City was a disaster. Any competent contractor knew not to count on the concrete truck arriving on time, so it was standard practice to order two loads from two companies. As the time for the pour approached, contractors would make a guess about which company was more likely to be there closest to the time they needed the concrete. Then they would cancel the other order. Now, to get the punch line, you have to remember that concrete cures in about 90 minutes. It does not accept requests to hold on for a few minutes. Once the water is mixed with the cement, sand and gravel in the back of the truck, mother nature's clock is ticking, and 90 minutes later the concrete must be out of the truck or you have a hardened-concrete-filled truck. For Cemex (and its competitors) this resulted in the cancellation of fully half of their orders on the day of delivery. This was a scheduling and logistical nightmare.

Now consider the anxieties present for the participants in this situation. The customers are anxious. They are contractors with slim margins, often paying interest on materials while constructing buildings, with crews ready and waiting, deadlines to meet to avoid unhappy customers or penalties. The salespeople are anxious. Their income depends upon their sales performance, yet they know to expect that half of their customers' requests will turn out to be cancelled at the last moment. The senior management are anxious. They know that these practices cause havoc and cost a fortune, but all efforts to repair the situation appear doomed to failure. The salespeople cannot avoid cancellations. A demand to customers to pay cash ahead only leads to customer defections. The finance people blame everybody, raise a continuous stink about the waste of money involved, and offer no proposals that can be implemented except to produce more controls and reports. Drivers and dispatchers appear victimized by the situation, but they are paid hourly, so they don't care. The whole thing leaves a big anxiety about an uncertain future.

'Virtuous' Anxiety

Our ungrounded anxiety offers two paths to the future. Anxiety can become a source of suffering in which we are 'thrown' (swept into automatic or habitual reaction) to attempt to eliminate or hide from the suffering it provokes. Alternatively, anxiety can be an announcement of our freedom as human beings. This is why we call it virtuous. Experiencing and acting on anxiety is an expression of human courage and autonomy. When a concern shows up, anxiety joins it and shows its face as an opportunity or invitation for us to design how we will live our lives. As we confront a situation in which there can be no true path, no absolute right way, we each have the opportunity to take responsibility for how we live[20].

Kierkegaard summed up the opportunity beautifully:

---

[20] Anxiety, Heidegger said, describes a sense of unease concerning the structure of one's life which, because it does not arise from any specific threat, is to be diagnosed as a manifestation of our own responsibility for this structure.

Learning to know anxiety is an adventure, which every man has to affront if he would not go to perdition either by not having known anxiety or by sinking under it. He therefore who has learned rightly to be in anxiety has learned the most important thing. – Søren Kierkegaard in 1844

A poignant example of the transformational opportunity of anxiety often occurs when someone faces death and survives. We have all heard stories of how people have a life-threatening illness and, during or after, drastically change the way they are living, their careers, their practices, and their hopes for the future. They may even find themselves joyful and grateful for their illness. They may find that they are able to reliably hold onto a sense of their life as an opportunity for invention, and able to commit to live it by design rather than by default as we often do.

From Anxiety to Action

Having unraveled somewhat the negativity and reactive emotional mess in which we are accustomed to interact with anxiety, we can now say something simple about it. Anxiety triggers us to wake up, to pay attention. That's the opportunity of it, the invitation of it. Something's changing. Wake up! Take a look! Make an interpretation! What happens is analogous to what a sudden noise or movement does to a sleeping cat. The cat comes to attention, surveys the territory, makes its equivalent of an assessment about what action to take, and then acts or goes back to sleep.

As we undertake to understand and make changes in our lives and circumstances, anxiety is an important diagnostic 'device.' Like an x-ray for the surgeon, or oscilloscope for the electronic engineer, fine distinctions about anxiety can allow us to observe 'hidden emotional structures and patterns' that underlie the ambitions, reservations, and resignations of the people who will be involved in a change. Those planning changes frequently make lists of the incentives and barriers to change. The incentives and barriers belong to the rational argumentation of change. The anxiety belongs to the background in which everyone involved is pulling for or fighting against a change.

Reliable interaction with anxiety requires more distinctions, as well as practice. To get into action, we need more than a new interpretation of anxiety; we need the interaction of biology and language.

Naming Possibilities for Action

Even before we distinguish that we are anxious or afraid, chemicals and impulses are moving through the body, producing sensations. The sensations trigger us, and we interpret that we are in or inhabited by an emotion – fearful, excited, anxious, serene, etc. As we distinguish our emotions, sometimes (but not always) naming them, they become 'real.'

People commonly understand our moods and emotions[21], including anxiety, through names we were taught in school as verbs (to fear), adverbs (fearfully), adjectives (a fearful thing), and nouns (fear). In

---

[21] In this paper we distinguish these two related phenomena that people usually treat as equivalents. Moods are relatively stable interpretations, held in our bodies, born in the past, that orient us to the future in a particular way. They tend to be shared in communities (by geography, profession, or culture, as in the moods of accountants, marketing people, researchers, the English, German, or French people, men or women), and to remain in our experiential backgrounds. (e.g., Many people agree: New Yorkers tend to have a general background mood of impatience. Ask a New Yorker about their impatience, however, and they typically will not understand what you are talking about. The mood is transparent to them.) Emotions are more volatile, associated with particular events, and tend to take over the foreground of our experience of the world. (e.g., "I was thrilled with the new coat"; "I fell in love.") If you lose your job you might find yourself in emotions of fear and sadness. If at the same time you are living in a generally optimistic or ambitious mood, you'll get past the emotions quickly and get into action finding a new job. On the other hand, from a generally pessimistic or resigned mood, you may sink into a depression, feel sorry for yourself, and be paralyzed for some period of time.

this tradition, we were taught and share the understanding that words are representational: the names are objects or things in written or oral constructions that in turn represent (point to or indicate) aspects of the reality we inhabit. Some of us may recognize that language is not merely representational but is the space in which meaning shows up in our world. Few of us, however, live as if this were the case. "In large part, most humans are commonsense Cartesians. We spend much of our lives struggling with the way things 'are', rather than savoring the malleability that a constitutive view of language, fully distinguished, might lend our world."[22]

We travel a non-Cartesian road in this paper. 'Language' does not refer merely to words, but to the understanding of things that accompanies the words. A powerful example of the role of language in creating the world is described by Hyde and Bineham from Helen Keller autobiographies[23]:

"Stricken at nineteen months by an illness which left her unable to see or hear, Keller was virtually without language and the understanding it makes possible. Writing of that period, she refers to herself as "Phantom," a "little being governed only by animal impulses...

---

[22] *Southern Journal of Communication*, v. 65, 2000: "From Debate to Dialogue: Toward a Pedagogy of Nonpolarized Discourse", by Bruce Hyde and Jeffrey L. Bineham.
[23] *Ibid.*l Photo courtesy digital.library.upenn.edu

. Her few words wilted [and] silence swooped upon her mind and lay over all the space she traversed" (Keller, 1955, pp. 37,41). Thus Keller was not merely wordless, she was worldless. "Before my teacher came to me," she writes, "I did not know that I am. I lived in a world that was no-world" (Keller, 1908, p.113). But when she was awakened by her teacher to the meaning-function of language, "the nothingness vanished" (Keller, 1955, p.42) and Keller was awakened simultaneously both to a self and a world.

"Human beings can inhabit only the world that has been distinguished in language by human thinking. The languaged world is, for human beings, the real world."[24] We introduced this earlier in the paper when we showed that the physical world exists in language, in our interpretation, and not in 'reality.' Moods and emotions, then, become real in language. We are calling them assessments here– one of six classes of language-action with which we invent, shape, coordinate and navigate ourselves and our world[25]. Assessments are evaluations, judgments, or opinions that we make about ourselves, our world, and our involvement in that world, in the interest of taking care of our concerns. When we make an assessment (I'm nervous; it's hot; she's smart; that car may pull out into my lane; I'm comfortable), we distinguish threats and opportunities, strengths and weaknesses, accomplishments and failures in domains that we care about. We are doing much more than naming or representing. When we make an assessment, we:

· Take stock of our world,

· Evaluate our progress, and/or

---

[24] *Ibid.*

[25] The six classes are *declarations, requests, offers and promises, assessments,* and *assertions.* We don't have space here even for a partial account of the extraordinary story of the discovery of language-action over the last 50 years. We'll introduce and use the distinctions we need in this paper and leave the rest for later. A good place to begin is Winograd and Flores' Understanding Computers and Cognition, 1987, Addison Wesley Professional.

· Prepare ourselves for action.

With each assessment, we make an interpretation, opening a space in which we can consider the possibility of action. For example, Shirah might make the assessment "The stock market looks very bad," and out of that assessment we might reconsider actions we took and plan new ones. Chauncey might say, "This article is too long," producing consternation (another assessment) as we push to get the paper ready to send to Design Club members.

As human beings, we make assessments all the time, frequently without noticing. When we do notice, we tend to think of our utterances as assertions — a second class of language-action. Assertions are facts that can be witnessed and tested for correctness or accuracy, rather than judgments or opinions that cannot be proven. 'Tall' is an assessment; 6'4" is an assertion. A score of 130 on an IQ test is an assertion that some would use to ground the assessment, 'smart.' "I am afraid" is an assessment; "that gun is loaded" is an assertion.

As we speak assessments, such as 'bad' and 'too long,' all too often we experience them in our bodies as truths, as assertions, rather than opinions. We react accordingly. We live in language, and our bodies can't tell the difference between assessments and assertions.

Even our assertions are founded in interpretations. Communities construct for themselves the capacity to make assertions by declaring language and standards for making the assertions and then institutionalizing those. We are able to assert that someone is 6'4" tall from a curious history. In thirteenth century England, King Edward I ordered a permanent measuring stick made of iron to serve as a master standard for the entire kingdom. This master yardstick was called the "iron ulna," after the bone of the forearm, and it was standardized as the length of a yard, very close to the length of our present-day yard. King Edward realized that constancy and permanence were the key to any standard. He also decreed that the foot measure should be one-third the length of the yard, and the inch one thirty-sixth.[26] This declaration has allowed us to observe and agree on distances reliably across witnesses. To support the measure, we have improved the stability of our standards, set up institutions to preserve them, constructed an industry of measuring device manufacture, and institutionalized education on the subject. Today, of course, all that is being thrown into a cocked hat in the US as we are moving to the metric system.

For more than 300 years we Western human beings have constructed ourselves as Cartesian realists and rationalists who can tell the difference between facts and opinions, reality and emotions. In this background, we continuously confuse and merge assertions and assessments. We experience ourselves as actors in a world of assertions – facts, including our own opinions, of course. On the surface, we forget that our assessments are judgments, interpretations, opinions. We ignore the fact that even our assertions are themselves founded in other interpretations. We 'forget' our fundamental ungroundedness. This posture allows us to build the appearance of a solid structure of reality in a world that lacks the solid foundations for which we seem to yearn.

Our bodies don't care about the elegance of our construction of this reality. No matter how much work we put into forgetting our ungroundedness and our anxiety, the anxiety continues to show itself. Apparently, this is part of being human.

Assessment Soup Pots

Like the soup pot that our grandparents used to keep on the stove, adding leftovers from today's meals, and taking out for tomorrow's

---

[26]http://www.cftech.com/BrainBank/OTHERREFERENCE/WEIGHTSandMEASURES/MetricHistory.html

meals, the body is an ongoing soup pot for assessments. It never stops generating sensations. Each new sensation is a fresh possibility for making an assessment: this is bad, that is good; this is cold, that is hot; I like this; I don't like that; your performance is poor; this project is going well; I'm uncomfortable with this; I'm satisfied with that. And, like the soup pot, each new assessment is put back into 'the pot' as part of the foundation for the next assessments.

The process happens so rapidly, so continuously, so transparently and habitually, that we normally don't distinguish between the sensations, the assessments, and the emotional constructions, much less between assessments and assertions. They appear smoothly, as a unified phenomenon. (Do you feel yourself getting anxious as you read this?)

We have described the process in this awkward way –"our bodies continuously produce opportunities for making assessments" – to make sure that we notice that 'the assessment' is an interpretation, and that you and I are the ones making that interpretation. Each of us is responsible for the way we 'design' our interpretations. We design them by commission – shaping and committing to an interpretation (pretty rare) – or by omission – accepting the interpretation that arrives to us automatically. One person's poison can be another's elixir. The physical sensations of sex are pretty much the same as those of fighting. Sensations such as fast heartbeat, sweat, and shortness of breath, are the same; what differs is the interpretation we make. The interpretation shows up in the way we talk about it. At a certain level, the body chemistry underpinning dread and incipient passion, or terror and high excitement, are very close to each other.

The Background of (Im)possibilities: Assessments, Moods, & Stories

All of us live in stories about ourselves[27]. We understand these stories to have been constructed by our 'experiences' but normally we pay little attention to what that might mean. Our stories are built in our 'soup pots' of assessments, without our realizing that we are constructing structures of assessments. We think of them as reported facts. The mechanism works in both directions, the stories reinforcing the assessments and the assessments reinforcing the stories. As we experience sensations, in a body moving through various affective states, the body 'invites' us to make particular assessments. By no coincidence, those states and assessments usually fit with 'our stories' about who we are and what we're doing. A teenager, confronting another low grade in school, concludes, "This sucks and I can't do anything about it. The teacher is out to get me. I can't win." In that moment, without noticing that he is doing it, he 'grabs' the sensations in his body and invents an extension of an old story of failure. As he does this, he reinforces and validates the old story – making it more solid and reliable – by showing himself that it is happening

---

[27] Photo of President Lyndon B. Johnson courtesy of CNN

yet again. Then, seeing his own 'wisdom' in the obvious and strong congruence between his emotional state and his story (again without noticing the machinery that is at work), he commits to the interpretation that this story is 'true.' This process is automatic – 'hard-wired' into our biology. It goes on nonstop, and for the most part, we are oblivious to it.

We suspect that every reader can find a good example of how people (including ourselves) hang onto and cultivate assessments that are shaped by the stories in which they have lived their lives. Let's come back to the example of Cemex that we introduced earlier.

The possibilities for acting in the world in which Cemex moved were circumscribed by a set of 'clear facts' that 'everyone understood.' The company's problems were caused by greedy customers operating in bad faith, the Mexican ("mañana") culture, horrible traffic in the big cities, drivers and dispatchers who didn't care, and an industry in which all of this was accepted standard practice. We can see now that these were assessments. From the middle of the actual situation, however, they were 'facts of life.' Of course each group of participants had their own slant on the situation, but the basic landscape of the interpretations was the same.

When Chauncey and his colleagues were invited to work with Cemex the company was dealing with this situation in the only ways that looked possible. They policed the behaviors of their own salespeople, drivers, dispatchers, and accounts receivable people in an attempt to work responsibly and with good practices. And they went after the customers, who, in the prevailing story, were the primary cause of the mess. The company organized their data to be able to distinguish 'good' customers. The company set up systems and a program to allow them to identify, at the moment of ordering, customers who had previously canceled orders on the day of delivery, and they were preparing themselves to enforce a policy that customers who had cancelled must pay cash ahead for new orders. They had only one big problem. The concrete business was no longer a monopoly, and had Cemex demanded that customers pay in advance, they would simply have gone to the competition.

What did we do? Starting with our clear recognition that our client was paralyzing and working against itself (including alienating and bullying its customers), we showed them the structures of concerns under their anxieties, taught them to listen to customers and key others, and worked beside them as they constructed a radical new practice in their company: delivering on time. When we were finished, they were able to promise their customers that if they failed to deliver concrete within ten minutes of the appointed hour, they would discount the order by 25%. Along the way, here are some of the key actions we took:

1. We recognized their anxiety. They were anxious in the obvious ways that anyone would be when their business is threatened, and in the deep ways that come with being human. Change is unsettling, and a gringo team bringing change to Mexico is even more unsettling. We didn't ignore that, nor did we try to reassure Cemex that all was well, nor promise we wouldn't make a big upheaval. We confronted the anxiety in the way we spoke with them and in the actions we took. In some ways we went to substantial effort to increase the anxiety. For example, we taught the Cemex design team to observe the anxieties of other people in the company, and together we produced a new diagnosis about what was really going on. Another example: we highlighted the high stakes of the game they were playing, and then transformed that anxiety-provoking-assessment into a virtue by showing them the opportunity for doing their whole business a new way that would produce a great deal more profit

and peace of mind. Another example: we reshaped their assessments and interpretations of customers from being the enemy to being their most important business allies.

2. We created serious opportunities for them to discover that their story was not the truth, and that a new, more powerful story was possible. The most important event turned out to be a visit to the dispatch center for 911 services in Houston, Texas, where they saw that it was possible to deal with customer requests that could not, by their nature, be anticipated, in very different ways than they had thought possible. It was clear to them that it was impossible to control the behavior of people calling for emergency services, and yet, we showed, the 911 dispatchers interacted with their customers with commitment. The Cemex design team got excited with the possibilities. Another example: We taught them to observe the interactions with their clients as coordinations of commitments (in which they co-invented, negotiated, and re-negotiated actions with the clients), rather than as structures of procedures (attempting to follow rules).

3. Of course there were many details about the process of design and implementation that we won't go into here. However, the most fundamental interpretations from which we guided all the work, day by day, had to do with anxiety and the way that listening happened. The result of the work? Ernst & Young, Accenture, and others have studied what we did, and called it 'best of breed' for that kind of process, and the work has been described in the Wall Street Journal, Wired Magazine, and several books.

Before we showed them a different relationship was possible, highlighted the consequences of their current way of working, and taught Cemex how to deliver concrete on time in Guadalajara and Mexico City, it had never entered their heads that it might be possible or even interesting to make and fulfill promises about the delivery of concrete in their major markets. When Cemex began to deliver on time, they found they saved $100s of millions each year.

Intervening in Stories: Assessments and Declarations

We have seen so far how the stories and assessments that we interpret as 'concrete' reality were shaped in the past, by earlier stories. They also can be re-shaped in the future by declarations (another class of language-action) that we make about how we're going to live our lives and conduct our business. With declarations, we create new distinctions in which to observe and act in our worlds. Successful declarations are effective. For those listening to and giving validity (or authority) to a declaration, it brings a new distinction around which all sorts of actions can be taken. Classic examples of declarations are The Declaration of Independence of the United States; declarations of marriage and of war; the naming of a new role, product, company, process, or child. In the moment that we have come to resolution that we are going to make some fundamental shift in our lives or the circumstances of our lives, the declaration is our most critical act. With declarations we invent something new. We will speak more about bringing new things into the world later in this paper.

The teenager of the last example can declare that he wants to make a good life for himself and a successful career. He can declare himself finished with his story as a loser, and can begin the construction of a new story, in which he builds competence and confidence in himself. Assessing that the old story doesn't work would be a step in the right direction, as would be making the assessment that a new story would be better; neither, however, is the same as making a declaration of a new beginning.

In the teenager's old story, he was open to being 'hooked' by all kinds of assessments about things he didn't like. Every glance of the teacher is meaningful. With the declaration that he is not going to succumb to the 'loser' (victim) story, he'll invent new interpretations. A low grade indicates learning is needed. If not an opportunity to be grateful for, it is at least an indicator of what is missing in his education. He may start noticing what he is doing as assessments spring forth from his body and mouth. He may be less inclined to interpret his own assessments as truths. Other interpretations begin to be possible. As he becomes more practiced, he may notice that he is a contributing author to the interpretations that are shaping his life.

The declarations that we make about our situatedness in the world often show up as moods in the background through which we interpret and act. If you have made effective declarations about seeing possibilities in life and yourself as effective, your background mood will likely be ambitious, and you will interpret daily events from that predisposition. You will tend to interpret bodily sensations of heart pounding, shortness of breath, and sleeplessness as excitement or anticipation. In contrast, if you have made declarations about life being devoid of possibilities, and yourself as a victim, your background mood will likely be resigned, and you would interpret those same sensations as fear.

Normal anxiety, as we are talking about it here, lives in the background of even such fundamental moods as these. The unsettledness comes upon us without respect for where we situate ourselves in life, announcing new possibilities or warning of new dangers, inviting us to consider the opening of the next new world, whether we want it or not.

Listen, Listen, and Listen

We are told that the correct answer to the question, "What are the three most important factors in real estate?" is "Location, Location, and Location." By analogy, in designing, listening is by far the most critical factor. To encounter anxiety in a rich way, then, we will first explore listening a little more, for it is 'in' listening that the encounter with anxiety and its parent, concern, takes place.

We have, however, some problems[28]. First, the standard interpretation of listening is about receiving and processing messages. We use tape recorders and computers as the model for understanding what we do!

After we move past this kind of interpretation, we find ourselves in 'deep water.' Whereas a geographic location is open to examination and charting, listening is hidden, and occurs in an uncharted domain. There is no discourse, no discipline, no serious literature, nor professors and students discussing the topic upon which we can build a structure of interpretations on which to stand to examine listening. Amazon lists over 1700 books with "listening" in their titles.

---

[28] Drawing courtesy of the US Air Force.

Only one serious philosophy book[29] stands lonely (and mostly un-read) on the shelves. Listening is a matter of concern in many fields, but, curiously, very rarely the subject of serious direct attention. Like Columbus embarking on his first voyage west in 1492, we go to sea in the world of listening without trustworthy maps to guide us.

With this background, we are interested in providing a way of think-ing about listening that can enable us to be more effective in taking care of our concerns, and the concerns of those we care about and are involved with. We are convinced that people can save time and effort, and go faster, if we have good distinctions in front of us as we are listening. It will be easier to motivate, train, and guide people into the new commonsense of what they are doing when we are in-troducing them to new practices. We will end up with designs that are more flexible. We will not be trapped so easily in rigid structures, and when we are, they will be less expensive to escape.[30]

As a point of entry to this conversation about listening, we recom-mend that you take a stand on listening: declare yourself ignorant and a beginner in the world of listening, or at a minimum, declare

---

[29] The Other Side of Language: A Philosophy of Listening, by Gemma Corradi Fiumara, 1990, Routledge. She has influenced us tremendously in our exploration.

[30] The picture, "Penguin Politics", from © SuperStock, Inc.

yourself to be without an adequate set of distinctions for navigating expertly in the world of listening. Commit yourself to attend to the phenomena and to learn about it. Commit yourself to a predisposition in which you make yourself available to have your way of knowing, your thoughts, and your emotions interrupted and altered by the process of listening to others. (Chauncey likes to say, with a twinkle in his eye, allow yourself to be damaged.) Usually, to risk less is not to listen.

Half of language – speaking – dominates our culture and our thinking about language. Our common sense treats listening as minor and passive, or, worse, a device in our arsenal of techniques for accomplishing our objectives.[31] When our business is bringing new human practices, however, listening must get the central role. Listening, especially listening to what we have not listened to before, is going to get increasingly important in this world, as change accelerates all around us. As we enter a community with a commitment to bring a change, it is our listening, not speaking, that brings us what we need for assessing, diagnosing, designing, and bringing new practices.

Everyone is listening, all the time, whether aware of it or not. In this sense, listening is a process of taking in, interpreting, and reacting. Listening is receptive, whereas speaking is assertive. Listening is gathering, whereas speaking is planting. Listening is quiet, while speaking is noisy. What would it be like, to walk around the earth just listening, not speaking? Take a moment to reflect on that possibility.

We are always listening, but we aren't in charge of how we listen. Before we enter into conversation with someone, we are already lis-

---

[31] What we have in our common sense as a basis for thinking about listening is a whole lot of talking about talking. There is almost nothing at all in our literature on the subject of what listening is about, really. One recent discussion that is better than most others is the social conversation about 'dialogue.' (At least in dialogue two parties are speaking!) Active listening shows us how to listen by speaking back what we listened; the technique has important limits. A number of professions, including especially psychotherapy, put a lot of attention on practices of listening, but these concerns are articulated as 'thinking', 'diagnosing', etc.; everything *but* listening.

tening in a particular way. Many listening techniques instruct us to become a blank slate. We bring you bad news: even at the moment of birth, we were already listening in a particular way. We are not – nor can we do more than aspire to be – open, impartial, empty vessels, objective, able to begin from a blank slate, nor able to stand in others' shoes. We are *structurally-determined biological systems*[32] that listen within structures originally laid in place literally millennia ago.

We acquire our listening from our historical, inherited ways of interpreting the world – historical discourses we embody from family, geographic location, gender, our prior experiences, and the historical events in which we live. Originally, we all absorbed these ways of interpreting uncritically, not noticing that they produced a particular way of interpreting the world. We assume our way is reality, the truth. For example, Shirah grew up in Brooklyn playing stoopball on stoops. Reminiscing about this with friends in our California home, she found people looking at her as if she were crazy. "What's a stoop?" they asked.[33]

We go about our lives deeply involved in our day-to-day activities, not stopping to consider whether what is obvious to us is obvious to others. It is only when we are able (or forced) to step back and observe our lives that we notice our listening. The exercise of attempting to step back can produce anxiety, too. It's always interesting to enter a new company and ask people why they do what they have been doing (usually without giving it much thought), for years, or to confront the jargon that people use without noticing that it is unique to their company.

---

[32] From Humberto Maturana and Francisco Varela, biologists who became dissatisfied with a biology that could make no sense of language and cognition except as metaphysical phenomena. They invented another biology with which we can understand language and cognition as biological phenomena. This is another topic for another moment.

[33] For those so unfortunate as not to have experienced stoops, they are the handful of stairs leading up to the porch of a house. Kids play stoopball by throwing the ball hard against the steps. It flies up into the air while they run backwards to catch it.

You are probably familiar with the claim of how Eskimos have more distinctions about types of snow[34] than those who don't interact with snow all the time. Consider, in contrast, the snow-distinctions of a skilled skier (fewer), or of a New Yorker watching the snow come down on his sidewalk (very few). The point of the more distinctions claim is to illustrate the connections among concerns, skills, distinctions, and the way we listen, comprehend, and interact with our world. You and I don't notice where we are Eskimos and where we are New Yorkers with respect to the essential distinctions in which we navigate in our own worlds. Our friend Matthew Budd tells a lovely story about himself as a novice doctor learning to use a stethoscope. It took him a long time to hear anything useful, because he didn't have the distinctions for listening. He describes the way that the doctor teaching him gently introduced him to listening over the stethoscope.[35]

We listen with our bodies, and our bodies listen to whatever they have experienced *that those bodies have distinctions for 'grasping.'* If we are missing distinctions and experience, however much we may want to 'think that we understand,' we do not. If we came from a family that prohibits the expression of strong emotions, we will not be able to make sense of anger or hilarity, and will feel intense anxiety when faced with them. Intense experiences get listened to over and over and over, whether we like them or not.

Speaking biologically, then, none of us is open; each of us is shaped by our heritage and experience, individually packaged, and we listen from those backgrounds and in the midst of the moods and emotions in which we live and find ourselves situated.

---

[34] It turns out that the claim of dozens or as many as a hundred Eskimo words for snow was, intentionally or not, a fraud. See http://www.aber.ac.uk/media/Modules/TF12710/vispero5.html or http://www.maa.org/devlin/devlin_2_97.html

[35] Matthew Budd, MD, You Are What You Say: The Proven Program That Uses the Power of Language to Combat Stress, Anger, and Depression, 2001, Crown Publishers.

Effectiveness Begins With Listening to Anxiety

Our orientation here is that listening is fundamental to what people do in life, and therefore to our capacity to design. It is fundamental to our successes and failures, in any domain you choose to look. Our ignorance of listening, and our incompetence with it, damages our capacity to understand, think, and communicate. Effective people are effective first as a consequence of their capacity to listen – to others, to themselves, to the condition of the world, to the implications of events and circumstances, to the space in which they are living. This is not to say that all effective people can articulate why they are effective. They may not be reflective practitioners of listening, even though they are quite good at listening. To move smoothly through a process of diagnosis, design, and implementation of a new practice, effective 'life designers' operate in very particular moods of receptivity, gathering, and quiet. They must be willing not to know what they have not yet seen, to be beginners at what they are to discover, and willing to be altered in ways that they cannot predict. These moods and postures will produce lots of anxiety. On the surface, anxiety appears an enemy of listening. With good distinctions and practice, however, anxiety opens, reinforces, and sharpens listening.

If we operate in the conviction that the anxiety (or the body sensations announcing it) is bad, or we declare that the emotion or sensations are 'wrong,' we stop attending (listening) to them. Some common methods are reassuring, denial, avoiding, and defending. We get busy doing what we know how to do, or we hunker down, waiting for the sensations to pass. Without realizing it, we muzzle our bodies, de-sensitizing ourselves to the capacity we have for attending (listening) to our bodies 'talking' to us. When we are anxious, our coping changes the way that we attend to others and ourselves. We put our attention on our anxiety, rather on what another person may be offering. Feeling anxious, we are frequently 'deaf' to the concerns of others, defensive or resisting them, anticipating and bracing ourselves against the change we sense coming.

Anxiety 'calls out to us' for comfort. Most of us have long since declared ourselves uncomfortable with anxiety, and when it presents itself we move to tranquilize ourselves or reduce the impending changes and risks. The inexperienced usually fall into this trap, and react by trying to make those around us comfortable. This is lethal to good design. Our anxiety tells us that something is or could be changing or shifting. It is up to us to determine and invent whether that is good news, an opportunity for us to practice our vocation, or some tragedy outside of our capacity to act.

Interpreting the Anxiety of Others

Now, here is another dimension of anxiety that's quite weird. Ask yourself how you actually come to the conclusion that someone you are working or living with is anxious. On the one hand, there is the rich language of the face and body. Some of us reveal more of our moods and emotions in our bodies and faces than others. As we get older, most of us mask our moods and emotions more carefully. Being 'too emotional' is politically incorrect. Thinking back, we can all remember moments when we were 'struck' with the interpretation that someone close to us was in a mood not revealed in their face or physical behavior. Further, many of us know people who have extraordinary skill at 'listening' to what others are not saying, or are feeling but not revealing. We'll say more about listening as a way of thinking about all this below.

It is easy to see that each of us interprets other people's emotional states from our own state. We interpret each other's emotional states 'through the lens,' if you will, of our own current emotional states. In other words, before I am interpreting your emotional condition, I am already in my own emotional condition, and that affects how I interpret yours. With anxiety, a great deal of the time, *I know that you are anxious because I feel your anxiety 'inside' myself.* We resonate with each other.[36] In Shirah's work as a spiritual director, she frequently experiences symptoms of anxiety in her body. When she was a novice, she attributed the anxiety to her lack of confidence in herself. With more experience, she has become aware that often her anxiety reflects the anxiety of her client. Today, before meeting with a client, she takes time to prepare herself, quieting her own body and 'interrogating' her emotional state. With this preparation, and a better interpretation of the current state of her own emotions and moods, she now uses her own anxiety as a signal that the client may be anxious, and works within that understanding. Conversely, if she interacts with the anxiety of others without good distinctions for distinguishing her own anxiety, she will have a cacophony of anxiety going on in her head/body, and no possibility of deliberately designing action. Worse, her client will be 'infected' by her anxiety, thereby damaging their work together.

Listening to Something New

Our final topic is perhaps the most important. As we commit ourselves to make changes, we play with boundaries and anomalies, inventing the new or different. *How do we listen to something new – to what we have not before listened?* Is the paradox obvious? How have we not been struck by it every one of our working days? Heidegger, we are told, laughed at all of us. He said, *It is unfortunate that*

---

[36] In their book A General Theory of Love (2001, Vintage Books), Thomas Lewis and his co-authors attribute this kind of communication to a phenomenon recently distinguished in brain research that they call *limbic resonance*.

we have the habit of listening only to what we already understand. Our challenge is to learn to listen to what we haven't listened to before (as well as to listen newly to what we have listened to before.) One of the critical skills is learning to listen to the difference between *assertions* that distinguish what already exists, and *declarations* in which the speaker is attempting to bring a new distinction.

Have you noticed what happens when you bring a new distinction to the table? Again, from Heidegger: *When we encounter something new, we normally say either, 'I know what that is; it is the same as this other thing that I already understand,' or, 'I know what that is; it is not very important.'*

We are immersed in standard practices that lead us in wrong directions. Aggressive clarification, strong questioning, insisting that the speaker make himself clear, and avoiding discomfort often are powerful misdirections. The moods of wonder and awe that are the appropriate moods for encountering 'the new' are politically suspect in adults. Instead we are trained to maintain the pretense that we know what we are talking about, looking good, not being a beginner. These are serious misdirections.

What does it mean to listen to what you haven't listened before? It means that you are participating in the invention of something. Once something has been invented, you can assert it. It can be described, defined, and reported; it becomes 'information.' Before it is invented, however, that which will be new exists only as a possibility. Often it takes a long time for things to move from possibility to being fully actualized. Cars were called horseless carriages for a long time before they became cars. The communications we make to each other over computers are still called 'electronic mail.'

During the period in which things become actualized, very often we appreciate only dimly or not at all what they are to become. In our modern era, increasingly we find things released while still in their design process. This allows those for whom they are intended to talk about them and participate in their invention. No one remembers Microsoft Windows versions 1 or 2; they were design releases. Windows version 3.1 was the first release that was used by a large number of people. Amazon.com now regularly showcases books before their writing is complete, which allows their authors to listen to and interact with the readers that could be interested in the books once completed.

As you listen, be willing for something that you do not immediately understand to happen – something unexpected or even unprecedented. This is where 'thinking out of the box' comes from. You cannot will yourself to 'think out of the box.' The place to start is with the discovery of the box in which you are already thinking. Appreciate and embrace the box, and then get interested in traditions, cultures, historical interpretations in which you do not already participate. Getting outside the box is not a capacity available to 'thinking' – in the traditional idea of thinking as analysis, speaking, aggressively articulating – it is something that happens in what we are calling listening.

Recommendations

The terrain we're beginning to lay out here leads to a whole series of recommendations for practices. We note some of them below.

1. Interrogate Your Own Anxiety

One set of practices that are crucial is what we call 'interrogating your own anxiety.' The point is to develop a good interpretation about what triggered the anxiety, and whether it is principally 'your own' or triggered by someone else. A structure for doing this is (a) notice your anxiety, (b) face it/surrender to it/embrace it, (c) invent actions from full responsibility for yourself and the situation. Let's go through each step.

a. Notice anxiety in your body reactions and your conversations

You cannot be balanced in life's conversations if you don't know how your own body responds to anxiety. If you are busy trying to shut down your body's reactions, you will waste enormous amounts of time. To attempt to avoid anxiety is to damage your sensory apparatus before entering the rest of your life. Instead, train yourself to observe your body reactions when they show up, observe the automatic interpretations you tend to make about them (I am angry, I am afraid), and observe the automatic, habitual actions you tend to take (get busy, get paralyzed).

b. Develop balance (face/surrender to/embrace anxiety)

Instead of your automatic practices to eliminate anxiety, you can choose to face it. Surrender to it, rather than resisting it. You can expand your capacity to dance with the anxiety, rather than running from it or ignoring it. (This counsel is for students and advanced practitioners as well. There is always room for learning in this.)

In facing anxiety, you acknowledge the precariousness and fragility of the human and organizational condition but do not succumb to dread. In essence you do not attempt to escape your own anxiety. You confront and deal with the existential challenges presented by crises that may affect your basic assumptions. This enables you to respond, and act more decisively.

Being balanced is not a form of unconsciousness, or unawareness resulting from tuning-out or covering-up anxiety. In fact, the same sensitivity that brought awareness of anxiety now informs you that you are free from the trap. Your mood on encountering the triggers to anxiety shifts towards wonder and openness. You can create a new interpretation of the symptoms - it is exciting, functional, surprising. Shirah remembers when she first read Heidegger's interpretation of anxiety. She was deeply relieved to discover that those vague feelings of dread and unsettledness that would come upon her at the oddest moments did not indicate there was something wrong that she needed to fix (and couldn't) but rather that it was simply a part of being human and an opportunity to design her life.

c. Invent from responsibility

Remember that we said anxiety shows up when something we care about is shifting. Ask yourself, what is it that I care about? What are my deep concerns? Is one of them being threatened? For example, Shirah realized in the process of working through her anxiety about the stock market that she had a deep concern about loneliness, expecting that as she aged she would become sick, alone, and lonely. She started to address this concern, rather than reallocating our stock portfolio (thank goodness!), and her anxiety about money began to dissipate.

Hard work alone will not bring this transformation; work very hard, and you might even inhibit its arrival. Our current interpretation is that the transformation comes out of opening yourself in three profound movements:

1. *Acknowledge your deep caughtness (along with all the rest of us) in the suffering of anxiety.*

2. *Give up your individualistic attempts to 'manage' or cast off anxiety.*

3. *Commit and surrender yourself to inventing a future in the midst of the anxiety.*

And, just as you don't become a salsa master overnight, you have to practice.

2. Produce Anxiety in Others

A second set of practices has to do with producing anxiety in others. Sometimes it is important that people for whom you care, and with whom you are working, become alarmed. They may not be taking care of something you think they need to take care of; or they may not have seen the implications of some change that is coming, or some unresolved situation from the past. In such cases, sometimes you need to provoke alarm, turning up the volume of their anxiety so they cannot avoid it.

Chauncey remembers a conversation with his father 15 years ago, in which he told his father, "You are making a terrible mistake moving into an over-55 community that prides itself on its rules to control the movement of children and other 'intruders.' You say you are doing this to protect your comfort. You're going to be comfortable for a long time after you're dead. The challenge right now is to design your life so that you are made *uncomfortable*, in the right moments, by the right things." Chauncey urged him to surround himself with grandchildren and other people he could not control. Their interruptions and requests to do things that he did not want to do, their pestering, and their messes would, he told his father, keep him alive and vigorous.

3. Diagnose Anxiety in Others

A third set of practices has to do with learning to diagnose anxiety-related behaviors in others. Are they fleeing into everyday busyness?

Do they wring their hands, schedule appointments, hire the fifth new advisor, run around, schedule more meetings, and so forth?

Alternatively, do they freeze, paralyzed, unable to make a decision, and analyze the situation to death? Do they complain and blame, but not act? Do they smoke cigarettes, go for a cup of coffee, spend time at the Xerox machine?

How can you help your clients observe their behaviors in the light of anxiety and listening? What people are seeking when they are fleeing into average everydayness is (and they'll explain this to you) to arrange a reliable structure for dealing with unpredictable, uncomfortable, unfathomable stuff. When they freeze, they are trying to avoid the whole mess, in the hope that stability will return if they just wait it out. Heidegger laughs at us about this too: *"This is foolishness. You will always fail (with these approaches)...."* There is no foundation from which you can construct reliable machinery for resolving, avoiding, or coping with the kinds of things that anxiety warns us about.

Let's think with an example. A client of Chauncey's asked the question, "What could go wrong?" in their project, and made a list of the risks they thought they would encounter – a long list. Then they had a long conversation with their clients about all the risks. Their client interpreted that they were just trying to protect themselves – 'CYA' in the jargon. The client responded by starting to negotiate how they, in turn, would avoid the risks, passing them back onto his client. For example, one risk on the list was that not enough people were assigned to work on the project. Chauncey counseled them to take the items on their list – many of them perfectly sensible assessments about the situation – and turn as many as possible into actions: requests to the client, offers to the client, or explicit promises that they undertook to fulfill themselves.

The uncertainty of life is the raw material of our work as designers of our lives and their circumstances. The nature of the human condition is essentially ungrounded, and that produces the opportunities in which we design.

4. Observe Your Own Listening

Each of us is predisposed to become anxious in some situations and not in others. We are triggered and listen in a particular way. The captain of the Titanic, we are told, literally went to sleep, unconcerned about the ice field dead ahead. Apparently, he was not anxious. He should have been. On the other hand, perhaps, he did listen, became anxious, and fled into arrogance, denial, or a false sense of security founded in the claims of the builders. The managers of the ill-fated launch of the Challenger Space Shuttle did not listen to the strong warnings of the engineers who had designed and constructed the boosters, requesting a delay of the launch. People today understand these and many other tragedies as failures of engineering, science, management, information, and psychology. We say no; first and foremost they were failures of listening.

Each of us listens in the background of our particular, idiosyncratic historical discourses. We should get to know these discourses and how they orient our listening.

5. Cultivate Moods and Structures for Listening

Take seriously the interplay of mood and listening. What moods can you cultivate to facilitate listening? Make yourself open and vulnerable. Be in a mood of wonder. Notice the norms among the people you work with. Are wonder and awe politically incorrect? (Almost always, yes….) How can you strengthen yourself so that you are not swept away by the common sense, others' moods, and the censure that attends politically incorrect moods? Speaking also affects listening. Train yourself and others to speak in ways that open, rather than close, possibilities.

In design conversations, ask, "What is s/he doing with what they are saying to me?" Listen to the entire historical discourse that is speaking out of the mouth of the person (or group) in front of you. If you listen carefully, you will hear a 'rational' surface of explanations, requests, assessments, and declarations, and, usually, an undercurrent in which the tradition to which they belong is speaking at the same time. The surface will be telling you what is wrong and how they want to fix it. In the undercurrent, you will hear the anxieties of their traditions speaking.

- "Whatever you do, do it fast, so we don't have to suffer the waiting."

- "Do something that doesn't appear too radical; our investors won't tolerate that."

- "Only a fool would suggest that we do something different than our competitors are already doing."

- "We've already tried everything; now we need to just do what we've been doing better than we have been."

- "Get rid of the CEO's (or CFO, etc.) anxiety first, or we'll never get the project off the ground."

- "Get rid of the employees' anxiety first, or they'll never tolerate a change."

Be vulnerable and willing to be changed, yourself. Be willing to be unsure, unpredictable, and confident, all at once. Listening is dangerous; our historical discourses are going to get threatened, broken apart, debunked. Are you willing for that to happen? If you answer 'yes', designs that bring new practices to our communities are possible.

We conclude with Kierkegaard. Our interpretation of anxiety stands on his shoulders:

> *That existential anxiety makes its appearance*
> *is the pivot upon which everything turns.*
> *in the state of innocence, we are not merely animals,*
> *for if at any time in our lives we were merely animals,*
> *we would never become persons of spirit.*
> *So spirit is present, but in a state of immediacy, a dreaming state.*
> *How does spirit relate to itself in this situation?*
> *We discover ourselves through existential anxiety.*
> *As spirit, we cannot escape from ourselves.*
> *Nor can we sink down into the vegetative life,*
> *for we are required to be spirit.*
> *We cannot flee from anxiety, for we love it;*
> *really we do not love it, for we flee from it.*
> *Our dilemma has thus reached its apex.*
> *We find ourselves in innocence and ignorance.*
> *But we are not brute animals,*
> *because even in our puzzlement, we are qualified by spirit.*
> *Our Predicament is precisely existential anxiety,*
> *in which we confront the immense **nothing**.*[37]

---

[37] Paraphrase by James Park based on two translations of a work by Søren Kierkegaard: The Concept of Anxiety, translated by Reidar Thomte (Princeton, NJ: Princeton University Press, 1980) p. 43-44, and The Concept of Dread, translated by Walter Lowrie (Princeton, NJ: Princeton University Press, 1944) p. 39-40.

Chapter 7: Navigating

Many years ago Fernando Flores offered a three-year-long program that he called the Ontological Design Course. In the world of philosophy, "ontology" refers to the study of being – how being comes to be, or how being shows itself. Those invited to the program had encountered Flores through his Communication for Action workshops and other courses he had offered. I had helped Fernando organize the program and eventually graduated from it myself. When the last group finished their third year, they decided to keep on meeting as "the ODC Community." They invited others who had done the program to join them, and they continue to meet periodically and have annual get-togethers to this day.

For many of the early years, I was an invited speaker for the community's events. This paper on navigation emerged from one of those. In the course, Flores acted as a strong coach. He spoke with what could be alarming directness to each of his students about what those of us schooled in the recent U.S. tradition of education had learned. We had been taught that we should always be nice to each other, that learning happens best when people are comfortable with each other, and that to be embarrassed by our failings was bad. As his chief of staff, I had long since learned that his assessments did not follow any party line and could sting when he spoke them. Whenever he would enter into a relationship with a student, he would go to work looking for how they might be able to be more effective in the world. He was relentless. And his students were, after his family and his commercial clients, those he cared for more than anyone else on earth.

As I approached this particular meeting with my fellow students I had grown tired of the self-satisfied mood of many of the ODC graduates. I thought that quite a few were missing the heart of the matter. I was irritated at what I took as shallow satisfaction with their growing familiarity with the work of various philosophers. They were not paying enough attention to the core commitments that Flores had brought to the program. So I prepared myself to scold my classmates and friends, and I produced this outline for a talk to the community.

As we had been students and friends together for many years, they generously granted me certain authority to speak in their midst, and they received my scolding with affection and care. We had a good conversation that lasted a couple of hours.

As the years passed after that event, I noticed again and again that I would return to these nine principles as relevant to conversations with colleagues, trainees, clients, and others. Even though 30 years have passed, they are still potent for bringing me back the whole of the interpretation of the world in which I stand. Every once in a while I would make a small adjustment in the wording of one or two of the points, but the document has turned out to be remarkably robust. It has stood the test of time. More recently, as I have been attending to what I have said that I want to make sure people listen to, this has become an important document.

Nine Principles for Navigating in our World

My mother, my father, Rose, Sibble, and Carnell Eaton[38] prepared me to listen to people including those very different than myself.

---

[38] See the introductory notes to Chapter 6 for an overview of who these people were.

Stafford Beer introduced me to Fernando Flores. Fernando Flores introduced me to:

- John L. Austin, his teachers, colleagues, and his student John Searle.

- Martin Heidegger, his teachers, his student Hubert Dreyfus, and his students.

- Humberto Maturana, his teachers, and his student Francisco Varela.

In this background, I have shaped the following nine principles for understanding how we human beings may navigate responsibly and effectively in our communities:

1. We are autonomous, caring, biological, historical, and linguistic beings.

2. We invent ourselves, our futures, our communities, institutions, tools, practices, and our understanding of all else in language. The kinds of beings we are live in language.

3. Our languages, our selves, and our communities are contingent and social phenomena.

4. Pervasive, ever-present moods and constantly changing emotions are constitutive of the kind of beings we are. Anxiety and unsettlement help us stay awake.

5. At the same time, what we listen to (and how we listen) are shaped by, and disclose the concerns, moods, and habitual ways of being that constitute us. We are creatures of habit, shaped by and shaping historical practices. (And we are far more malleable than the prevailing common sense would suggest.)

6. Entrenched, archaic, and impoverished interpretations about what human beings are, about what it is to be human, and about what we do with each other contribute strongly to the difficulties we have in coordinating with each other.

7. We take stock of ourselves and our worlds, notice changes, and open possibilities for action with assessments and assertions. We take responsibility for constructing our futures by making requests, offers, promises and declarations. Some call these language-actions.

8. Our worlds and enterprises are constituted as networks of commitments that emerge through our conversations.

9. Design is the name I give to the practices of building bridges to alternative futures.

Chapter 8: The Manifesto

From the time I started working at Arthur D. Little, Inc. I began to understand that the heart of my work had to do with finding different ways to observe and act in our worlds. The manifesto is a formal rhetorical device that has the role of helping people living in one world (that is, in an era, a particular paradigm, community, country, tradition, or discipline) to make a transition from that world to another (partially or largely new) world. The idea that we bring a new situation into the world by defining missions and objectives and planning projects to get there is good for inventing new things within your current world. It doesn't work when the task is to move to a different world. There, we have not yet arrived at a place from which we can view the new world. What we have clear is the shape of the old world, the world with which we are currently dissatisfied.

Over the years I have repeatedly found myself inviting teams to produce a manifesto as they confronted the challenge of making a jump from their current world to a new one. Examples that come to mind are 1) Cemex as they learned to deliver concrete on time in Mexico City and Guadalajara and 2) Scottish and Southern Energy as they moved to make massive changes to their design of distribution systems and move rapidly ahead with an investment of 10 billion pounds in renewable energy systems.

Fernando Flores and I invented this rhetorical device in a conversation. It serves me as an example of what he means when he says that he and I have been working together for so many years now that it is impossible to tell where he ends and I begin.

After I introduce the eight parts of the manifesto below, I have included as an example one of the great manifestos of the modern world – the Declaration of Independence of the newly emerging United States. More about that when I get there.

The Manifesto

Structurally, the declaration that we recommend that you and your team construct follows a logic we call "the manifesto." This is a rhetorical logic we built many years ago for constructing a document (or speech, or other complex 'illocutionary' action) that has the objective of helping a community prepare themselves to make the 'trip' – the transition, transformations, and changes that are required to move the community from one world to another. The point is to enable a community to change the perspective from which it observes a situation or world to enable it to:

· Break historical *resignation*,

· Establish the basis for an authentic *conviction* for working in a new way towards building a new world, and

· Define certain of the fundamental distinctions that will be used for building a bridge to a new world.

Resignation is the term we give to a habitual predisposition found to some extent in all large organizations. In the predisposition, the mood of resignation, people listen, act, and interpret the world as if many things that are in fact within their capacity to affect are completely outside of their control. We look for historical resignation in the cultural style of company, in its industry, the communities it serves, and in the dominant discourses employed in running the business (e.g., engineering, financial management, and other disciplines and discourses).

By *conviction*, we mean to distinguish a predisposition or pre-orientation quite different from hope, courage, or intentionality. Rather, the manifesto structure is designed to guide work to lead to the construction of a grounded narrative that will be used for organizing investment conversations and the design of work. Conviction can be built from – grounded or founded in – various sources. People can find themselves in a state of conviction because their narrative about the future is built on top of long-established historical discourses that explain how the world works the way it does. Gravity belongs to the discourse of physics, and lets us be confident that, released at some altitude above the earth, things that don't fly will fall. To be convinced that a space shuttle will successfully launch, we need to found our conviction upon physics and chemistry, other discourses like computer science and digital communications, and also on less-well-grounded narratives about how human beings can work together reliably.

We can build conviction that certain cost-cutting activities are going to raise the profits of a company, but experience also tells us that narratives that explain such things as profits may have the capacity to give foundation to new stories about bringing value (e.g., shared services and outsourcing), but the results do not follow automatically from the stories.

From a new understanding of your capabilities and how those allow you to deal with emerging situations and concerns, you can build conviction. From emerging alliances in an industry or a country that are shifting the balance of power in industries or regions of a country, you can develop conviction that things that were before not manageable will begin to be manageable.

The manifesto forms a foundation for the entire process of understanding, planning, and mobilizing a change, including the habits (emotional and intellectual structures) in which the old and new world, and the process of navigating between them, can come to be understood by the community.

Writing a declaration, and following the logic of the manifesto for doing that, is not an exercise in incendiary speaking. The manifesto and the declaration that emerges from it will reveal the historical style of the company, including what those responsible for bringing a new world appreciate about it, and what they will attempt to rebuild. Nor is the process some kind of scenario planning – as in revealing what Peter Schwartz calls the Inevitable Surprises (see the book of the same name).

The manifesto will put those responsible for crafting the declaration in touch with the fundamental fact that the world is invented in conversations. The manifesto needs to produce a moment of authentic listening and thinking; it is valuable when it produces a moment for the community to own themselves in an authentic way.

Finally, the manifesto is not so much an outline for writing, but an outline of the structures that need to be dealt with in writing the declaration.

The eight parts of a manifesto:

1. Declare the essential 'breakdown'

This is an articulation of the central problem and opportunity (they usually appear together) that will be in the center of your design.

A good story for thinking about what this might mean comes from the invention of the vaccine for anthrax developed by Pasteur at the end of the 19th century. At the time, the disease was understood as a scourge of god – something completely outside the world of possible action by human beings. When the scourge hit, what people saw was a lot of cows dying suddenly, and the situation did not respond to prayer, magic, or any of the other things that desperate farmers applied. In France at the time, the farmers were the most sophisticated dairy farmers in the world. When the scourge hit, the problems to be dealt with were burying dead cows and growing more of them fast when they died. The dead cows were inescapable.

Pasteur made a radical interpretation: the 'breakdown' that he put his attention on – problem and the opportunity together – was the actual dying of the cows, and he proposed the radical solution of keeping the cows alive. There were many reasons why this possibility did not occur to the farmers of the time. There was no common sense about bacteria (Tiny invisible little animals that could kill big animals? Ridiculous!) The farmers were at the top of their field, and suffered from the great curse of being on top of a field. They were arrogant and had the cognitive blindness that accompanies arrogance. And no small part of the reason that the farmers did not confront the central issue – dying cows – was connected with the fact that they cared about the cows. Like surgeons trained "not to get too close to patients," the farmers had built habits of interacting with the death of the cows that allowed them to escape suffering at their deaths.

Closer to home, the invention of SDO (on-time delivery of ready-mix concrete) at Cemex Mexico in the early 90s shows another good place for understanding what is happening in this part of the manifesto. At the time that we began to intervene, half of the orders of the ready-mix business in Mexico were being cancelled on the day they were scheduled to be delivered. The reason? Contractors did not trust the suppliers to deliver on time, so the standard practice was to order from two vendors and then cancel the one you thought was likely to be later. For all the people involved, drivers, dispatchers, customers, salespeople, executives, finance people, and so forth, the truth of the situation was self-evident. With the lack of concern for on-time performance of the Mexican culture, the extreme variety of demand, the traffic in the main cities, and the 'poor' quality of the labor forces, the unions, the greedy customers, and so forth, there was no way to do anything about it. Some of us convinced those responsible that stopping sales to customers with a record of cancellations who did not come down and pay cash was simply a way of investing in helping competitors' sales. The breakdown around which we organized the design team for the SDO project was in the idea that it was impossible for Mexicans to make and reliably fulfill promises under such circumstances. It turned out, as we expected, that building that capacity – previously understood as just as impossible as stopping the deaths of the cows in the late 1800s – produced and continues to produce many hundreds of millions of dollars in new revenues and cost savings every year.

2. Warn about the limitations of the obvious solutions

These are the solutions that people are already assuming will shortly or eventually take care of the problem for them.

When dealing with big problems there are always a few 'obvious' solutions that keep peoples' blindnesses in place. Typical examples: other people smarter than me are working on the solution; technology will come along that deals with it.

3. Denounce the misconceptions underlying the resignation

Resignation stays in place in part because of underlying misconceptions that produce much of the complexity, confusion, and mess surrounding the current interpretation of the situation. These misconceptions claim, in effect, that nothing more can be done about the situation.

These will be stock misconceptions of the era, the industry, the main discourses that define how the industry and business work, and so forth.

4. Introduce a new clearing (world)

Here you will announce – declare – that you are going to bring a new world. You will not know completely, or perhaps much of how you will do that, but, as in the case of John F. Kennedy's announcement that the US was going to put a man on the moon in 10 years, you dare to announce your commitment to dissolve the complexity and produce a new interpretation and 'solution.'

For example, in the Cemex case, we started by dissolving the current interpretations about the shape, destiny, and key drivers of the cement and concrete industries in the US and Mexico, and beginning a new construction by examining the kinds of roles that concrete can have in the practices of the people of the country over the coming decades.

5.   Introduce the key operational distinctions

In the case of my work over the last 40 or so years, language and the way that we human beings invent our futures in language have been recurringly important distinctions that I have employed for dissolving problems, taking advantage of opportunities, and producing plans of action.

For other examples, listening, a new interpretation about who our customers are, how we will interact with them, and a new set of distinctions about the roles of managing and leading, will be constructed to shape a new set of capabilities for the new world.

6.   Define the overall program

This is the place for outlining and beginning to lay out the big proposal for moving to a new world.

7.   Define your priorities

What are the main pieces of the puzzle, and which parts will need to come first.

8.   Make requests and offers

Here you begin to put the team into action by making offers and requests for actions now and in the near future for launching the project and its parts.

The Declaration of Independence

On July 4, 1776, 56 men signed the Declaration of Independence. This was a classic manifesto, executed at the moment that the colonies in the "new world" realized that they needed to move to a new world. Examining its structure, main elements, and the results it brought illustrate many things about what we are talking about here.

In the first image, below, I have copied the entire text of the original declaration into tiny type so that I could fit it onto one page. We are not going to be reading it here. I do recommend reading it, but not here. You can read the document on the Internet.

I have color-coded the text into its three major parts, which I have summarized in the second image. Notice that the color coding covers the full texts of three major parts of the text, so that we can get a sense of the weight given to each part: the declaration of the kinds of people we take ourselves to be, the complaint against the King of England and his minions (and against ourselves for taking so long to orchestrate our complaint), and the declaration and promise that the 56 made in this declaration.

> We declare our interpretation of the world, who we consider ourselves to be, and the standards to which we will hold ourselves.
>
> **We make a serious, grounded complaint against those we have been following for (1) not listening to and acting upon our proper requests, (2) many actions they have taken without concern for our well-being, and (3) the damage and suffering produced by those actions (and against ourselves for having taken so long to act.)**
>
> We declare a new order, and in support we promise "our lives, our fortunes, and our sacred honor."
>
> © Copyright 1998, Business Design Associates, Inc. All rights reserved worldwide. 8/98   22

Important things about this document do not follow the logic of modern, technological and engineering-style proposals that we build to bring new initiatives and important changes. Look at how much of the document is its complaint! Teams attempting to change the direction of companies and communities run right past the crucial opening moments of the manifesto, diving into the action of the project. In doing so, they rush past the critical opening of the job. As I laid out in *My Problem With Design*, the first part of the job of bringing something new is constructing and putting in place the structure of provocations. The provocations emerge primarily from the complaints. Why should those invited to participate in bringing a new world give a damn? Why should they invest themselves in this new possibility? Changing is expensive, and risky, and calls on those leading those changes (and those who will be affected by the changes) to step forward – to 'take a stand' – and to put themselves in the line of fire that always accompanies attempts to bring change. The idea that we make important changes through consensus, "buy-in," or other popular management jargon is nonsense. There are always, and always will be opponents, people who do not want or support important changes. Important changes bring shifts in identities, in power, in flows of capital, and in our ways of being in the world.

In the Declaration of Independence there is no vision, no statement of mission, no objectives, no plan of action, no budget, no forecast of increases in capital that will be produced. It says that the speakers interpret that they are a particular kind of people; that they are fed up and that the current situation is ending now; and that the speakers promise their lives, fortunes, and sacred honor to that end. By far the largest part of the document is concerned with the complaint about the situation that the manifesto is constructed to help leave behind. The documents shaping the action – the Federalist Papers, the Constitution, and others – they came later, after the gauntlet was thrown down.

I cannot pass by this moment without noticing the parallel to the current turmoil in the United States, in the third quarter of 2020, where the Federal Government is sending armed military forces into cities led by political opponents of the current administration to suppress demonstrations by people complaining about situations that parallel those of the late 18th Century. Perhaps the irony here includes that the Brits were dressed in red coats, clearly identifying them as the people representing the authority of the British government, and in the US the Federal forces today are fully anonymous, driving unmarked and unlicensed cars, without identity on their uniforms.

What kind of people were the signers of the Declaration of Independence? Some were major figures in their communities; others were 'normal' people. Twenty-four were lawyers and jurists. Eleven were merchants, nine were farmers and large plantation owners; men of means, well educated. But they signed the Declaration of Independence knowing full well that if they were captured the penalty would be death. (The following is thanks to Wikipedia.)

· Five signers were captured by the British, charged as traitors and tortured before they died.

- Twelve had their homes ransacked and burned.

- Two lost their sons serving in the Revolutionary Army, another had two sons captured.

- Nine of the 56 fought and died from wounds or hardships of the Revolutionary War.

- Carter Braxton of Virginia, a wealthy planter and trader, saw his ships swept from the seas by the British Navy. He sold his home and properties to pay his debts, and died in rags.

- Thomas McKeam was so hounded by the British that he was forced to move his family almost constantly. He served in the Congress without pay, and his family was kept in hiding. His possessions were taken from him, and poverty was his reward.

- Vandals or soldiers looted the properties of Dillery, Hall, Clymer, Walton, Gwinnett, Heyward, Ruttledge, and Middleton.

- At the battle of Yorktown, Thomas Nelson, Jr., noted that the British General Cornwallis had taken over the Nelson home for his headquarters. He quietly urged General George Washington to open fire. The home was destroyed, and Nelson died bankrupt.

- Francis Lewis had his home and properties destroyed. The enemy jailed his wife, and she died within a few months.

- John Hart was driven from his wife's bedside as she was dying. Their 13 children fled for their lives. His fields and his gristmill were laid to waste. For more than a year, he lived in forests and caves, returning home to find his wife dead and his children vanished. A few weeks later, he died from exhaustion and a broken heart.

· Norris and Livingston suffered similar fates.

My friend Stephen Tobias speaks of a passage in Eikev, a chapter in the Torah, as an "attempt to drive home the idea that *we have, as individuals and as a people, choices to make, and that from these choices follow immediate and profound consequences (even if it takes time for us to see them).*"

We have choices to make. As the world turns, day by day, the circumstances of our lives open and close contingencies, moments in which we can choose paths of action, or paths of inaction. The best paths for ourselves and those we care about are not always paths for actually taking action. Inaction, patience, waiting and watching, and the mood of emotional fortitude that Fernando recommends people cultivate – these are also important. My mother of blessed memory, Katharine McCulloch Scott, built a good part of her life around her own version of the words of Isaiah: "Help me find the courage to change the things I can, the serenity to accept the things I cannot, and the wisdom to know the difference." She was my first, and in the end, most important teacher.

What choices are you called to make? What has your path in life been aiming you at? What networks do you belong to? With whom have you been working, building or singing?

Is it time for you to begin to craft a manifesto to help yourself or those you care for make a transition from one world to another? To build a bridge to alternative futures?

Moving Forward

Thank you for investing in this conversation with me.

In closing this first volume, I invite you to join a community of people who are exploring the practice of building new practices.

Each of us is surrounded by people, communities and organizations who could benefit by building new ways to navigate the ever-growing contingencies of our worlds. In my experience working with people and organizations, building this competence begins with listening. When we listen deeply – that is to say when we pay serious attention to what is happening – what can we discover? What can we learn listening more carefully to others, ourselves, and what is happening in the clearings in which we live?

In former times when things were not changing so rapidly, we could rely on established paths and habits – existing ways of working and being. Not now. In the era we have entered, the bell of change calls on us to continuously adjust our plans, directions, and horizons. We even have to adjust our understanding of ourselves, our opportunities, limits, and ambitions. The COVID-19 pandemic is only the latest director on the stage. Many voices are telling us what deserves our attention. In some cases, wise voices are making assessments to which we should be attending carefully; many others are exercising their right to have opinions without care, and we need prudence and caution.

· Our 'mobile phones' are tiny supercomputers with video cameras and portable theatres connecting us to global networks. Each day these 'phones,' the Internet and our computers introduce new vistas, disrupting and altering how we engage in relationships with other human beings.

· We have lessons daily from our media. The 'news' is not about what is novel and deserves our attention; we are being trained in destructive ways of listening and speaking. It is time to move away from our fascination and habitual attraction to the 'news' and begin serious preparation of new narratives to underpin how we understand what is going on around us.

· Many of us have settled into contentious styles of public and private interaction. These styles have not gained traction through our personal choices. Rather it is the 'clearing' I discussed in chapter 2 that is managing the backgrounds to which we all belong. The clearing shapes our listening and attention, and builds walls indiscriminately in families, neighborhoods, communities, states, and countries. Avoiding being managed by the clearing takes serious attention and effort.

· The vast and widening gulf between the haves and the have-nots is not merely a fact; it shapes what is available to us and how we think of ourselves and others. Our growing recognition of how we have ignored, mistreated and damaged many 'others' in our worlds – women, people of color, disabled people, people from other traditions, *and those we don't want to listen to* – either move us towards new kinds of self-isolation or challenge us to cross personal bridges.

By joining with others who are also committed to learning, we can generate power to influence our worlds. If you are fortunate, you may be able to participate in the design of worlds more satisfying for us and the generations to follow.

If you or a client of yours has a practice to build, we offer design. If you are an executive, a board member, consultant, lawyer, investor, are guiding an enterprise and find yourself entangled in a thicket, we can help you find your way out and into the process of building new practices.

Take Action!

Dancing in the World is the first volume in the Mobilize series. Become a member of our community of business designers, consultants, thinkers, and philosophers building bridges to alternative futures. Register below to be notified about future volumes, to find out about educational opportunities, or to talk with us about projects where you would like our assistance.

Contact us at www.harvester.academy

Holiday – [illegible]

– [illegible]

Printed in Great Britain
by Amazon

51511614R00113